THE BOYS OF SPRING

THE BIRTH OF THE DODGERS

D1606684

ALLEN SCHERY

DEDICATION

To my uncle Paul Denais who came back from World War 2

and got me interested in Baseball and to Gil Hodges who loved

all the kids

.

ACKNOWLEDGMENT

On August 4th, 1997, Tommy Lasorda was inducted into the Baseball Hall of Fame. Across the street from the Hall, I attended a celebration party. At the party, I met Roger Kahn, who authored "The Boys of Summer" about the 1950's Brooklyn Dodgers. We spent the entire night discussing Dodger History to the consternation of everyone else who wished to speak to us. As a salute to him and because my book is about the origins of the Dodger Baseball team, I chose the "Bookend" title "The Boys of Spring."

PREFACE

Writing a treatise like this requires the following clues. It is like a detective novel, but no one can be questioned in this case, as they all passed away many decades ago. One arrives solely with value judgments and the weighing of evidence. When we get near the edge, we get into the area of guessing, which is dangerous and undesirable. Most academics like to play it safe and quote the quotes so they cannot be intellectually attacked. It is far more interesting to speculate to the best possible interpretation, which is how I like to write. I will add the caveat that I will change my understanding considering any new data as any devotee of the scientific method would do. I have no Holden Caulfield like in J. D. Salinger's "Catcher in the Rye" to save me from going off the edge. The only way to get to the facts is to dig up every possible clue (which I spent endless hours doing) and present them in the most logical, cohesive manner. I will give notes at the end of this discourse to show where some of my interpretations first saw the light. Much of the data comes from old newspapers, and many errors I have seen come from faulty memories and defective or lousy reporting. In many cases, three or more different stories have emerged. When journalists must publish in one day, there is not much time to research, be analytical, and check out sources. Unfortunately, these are the only scraps left. However, it makes the story even more enjoyable! Remember, this is Baseball history, and few at the time thought any historical work like this might ever be done. After all, it is just a sport. Right?

TABLE OF CONTENTS

INTRODUCTION

If we go back to the dawn of modern man, we will undoubtedly find the usage of sticks and stones. Suppose you recall Stanley Kubrick's 1968 landmark movie "2001 a Space Odyssey" based on the philosophies of Kierkegaard, Heidegger, and George Bernard Shaw, including a book by Arthur C. Clarke. In particular, we find a section on "The Dawn of Man." We viewed our ancestors' throwing rocks at each other from opposing sides of a waterhole. In contrast, one group figured out how to club members of the other group on the head. So, you see, Baseball may be primal. We have only substituted balls and bats for stones and clubs!

Baseball may be a modern-day substitute for warfare and judging by the behavior of some of the fans still a form of physical contact and violence, at least in the minds of the lunatic fringe.

According to uniform rules, the idea of batting a ball with a small, round club did not appear in any dim version. Ball games of countless kinds were well known to the Egyptians, Greeks, and Romans. It was even true amongst the ancient Maya in the Yucatan, but they would sacrifice the winning team to their gods as a reward, no less!

The custom of hitting a ball for distance, as in cricket and Baseball, did not arise in the past because they could not make a ball; they could drive a long way. When a sport calls for a ball to be hit, it is done by hand or racquet. It existed in tennis and badminton, where a shuttlecock is knocked back and forth with a small racquet. Such activities flourished all through the Middle Ages. They were joint recreations seen on village greens, but football (soccer) was even more common recreation on village greens; football (soccer) was even more popular with the masses in those bygone days. That was because it was easier to make a large ball, they could kick around than a small one solid enough to be smashed for distance.

This is true with a Baseball, as still earlier, it had fashioned a ball for cricket. The arrival of a suitable kind of shaped ball, which in turn gave rise to an appropriate Baseball bat, led to the origin of hitting something far enough to reach a base. The latter never advanced beyond going back and forth between two bases, while Baseball became prominent with three bases and a home plate and hitting for distance.

Baseball, as distinguished from a mere pastime or something to spend time at, came into being with the organization of the New York Knickerbockers in 1845. However, the Knickerbockers had been combined in a type of loose organization since 1842 for practice purposes only.

Alexander J. Cartwright invented the game and gave it a purpose when, after an afternoon on the diamond in the spring of 1845, he proposed signing players for each club. Initially, we see these teams as banquet and whisker teams as they played for the reward of banquets and had severe acreage of hair on their faces.

Raconteurs of those days fail to tell us whether in a close decision a runner was out making a head-first slide if the fielder put the ball on his whiskers, or in making a fall-away slide from the front, was a man safe if his whiskers were on the bag while he was still a foot away from the bag? We will never know!

In the summer of 1846, they played the first game in history at the Elysian Fields in Hoboken, New Jersey, between the Knickerbockers and a team called the "New York's." The reward was a good dinner for all, and we never heard of the "New York's" again. Some claim this to be the origin of Baseball, not the Abner Doubleday/ Cooperstown myth created half a century later. Some say the Baseball Hall of Fame should be in Hoboken, New Jersey others say, Prospect Park, Brooklyn.

I am sure one could draw other conclusions based on the considerations one would use. Things don't always have exacting delineated points to draw on. There are many ways to parse the data or invent it.

The Knickerbockers; uprightly adorned the diamond and the festive banquet board for thirty years. They firmly established Baseball as the game played today. It was then known as the New York Game of Base Ball, while townball, which thrived in New England, was known as the Massachusetts Game of Base Ball. Brooklyn was a little slow in getting into the new line of just the athletic endeavor because banquets of the quality seen were quite addictive.

The Washington Club changed its name to the Gotham Club, which was more appropriate, and in 1854 came the Eagles and the Empire Base Ball Club, both of New York. That gave New York an emerging league of four clubs the Knickerbockers, Gotham's, Eagles, and Empires. Here are the clubs ascribed to Brooklyn three years later in 1857: The Excelsior's; South Brooklyn; Putnam's; Williamsburg; Eckford; Greenpoint; Atlantics; Jamaica; Continentals; Star; Hamilton's; Brooklyn and Mutual. That was not a bad showing for Brooklyn, which soon became a force felt on the diamond.

1858 saw the first Baseball game, where they charged an admission fee (50 cents). That first game was played at the Fashion Racecourse, Long Island, on July 20, 1858, between picked nines from Brooklyn and New York. It gave the professional game its first stimulus. Whether $750 was blown for a banquet is not stated, but the time of feasts was about to become extinct. They betted heavily on the games, and even then, the habit of gamblers giving money to players who made a hit or a play that won a bet existed. It should come as no surprise given the nature of man.

The next revolutionary step credited to Brooklyn was the Excelsior club of 1860, which took on teams from Albany, Troy, Buffalo, Rochester, and Newburgh on a pioneer road trip. They then took on teams from Pennsylvania, Delaware, and Maryland, beating all comers.

They returned home victoriously and saw a challenge from yet another team from Brooklyn known as the Atlantics. The first two games were split, with the Atlantics barely beating them in game two by a 15-14. The third game broke up in a riot showing how crazy "cranks" (called fans today) could be.

The first recorded championship of the association was the Eckfords beating the Atlantics for a title in 1862. The team's star first baseman Al Reach later became the well-known head of a sporting goods firm bearing his name.

In 1864, he was offered money to join the Philadelphia Athletics. He did and became the first professional Baseball player in history. The Eckfords also went unbeaten in 1863. The

Atlantics finally caught up to them and won in 1864 & 1865, unbeaten both times.

Al Reach

The first enclosed ballpark was the Union Capitoline Grounds, located at the corner of Muncy Avenue and Heywood Street in Brooklyn (a National Guard Armory now stands there). Immediately, history was made there when a pitcher named "Candy" Cummings for the Brooklyn Stars threw the first known curveball (though it has seen debate). Scientists then called it an optical illusion, but in unmistaken Brooklynese, the Atlantics players cried out, "We seened it."

In 1865, a visiting player named Eddie Cuthbert from the Philadelphia Keystones, possibly caused by the news from Appomattox Court House, took off and "stole" second base. A growing fight was in progress on the field as the team captains waved their hands up and down while others ran for the rule books.

The cranks in the wooden stands were virtually in hysterics at the sight of a ball player throwing himself in the dirt. Umpires had to be careful back then as "cranks" could wait to attack them after a game if their ruling was unfavorable to the home team. The result was that there was no rule prohibiting Cuthbert's actions, and as there was no tag, he was deemed safe at second. Ergo we have the birth of the first stolen base happening in Brooklyn.

Not to be left out, the Atlantics came up with some histrionics of their own the following season. Dickey Pierce of the Atlantics deliberately reached out with his bat and gently touched the ball into fair territory. Pierce had just invented the bunt! He then ran to first base safely while the opposing team stood there like stunned deer in the headlights.

While the Civil War checked the growth of Baseball in some ways, it advanced the game by leaps and bounds. It was played by soldiers of both the Northern and Southern armies. Whenever they had the opportunity, prisoners in stockades played. The result was that brigades from States that had hardly heard of Baseball became acquainted with it in camp, and when they returned home, the discharged soldiers taught their friends the game.

Among those who learned the sport In the Northern Army was Nick Young. He became a famous outfielder and, some years later, the president of the National League. Albert Goodwill Spalding, whom we all know, is associated with a Baseball, put Nick Young's name on a Baseball.

Until 1869 Baseball was "supposedly" a purely amateur sport though crossings of the border between amateur and professional Baseball could still be found and documented to varying degrees.

Albert Spadling   **Nick Young**

In 1869, the Cincinnati Red Stockings became the first all-professional Baseball club. They then started a long winning streak that almost reached two full seasons. That was, of course, until they came to Brooklyn and met up with the Atlantics at Union Capitoline Grounds. After nine innings, the score was tied. In the 10th inning, Cincinnati scored 2 runs, but in the bottom of the 10th, Brooklyn came out and scored 3 runs to win the game and end the Red Stockings' winning streak at seventy-eight games. The Red Stockings disbanded that same fall in 1870.

Brooklyn Atlantics defeated Cincinnati Red Stockings on June 14, 1870

Another matter of note from Brooklyn Baseball history came with a Hall of Fame Sportswriter named Henry Chadwick, who reported Baseball from the Civil War right up until he died in 1908.

HENRY CHADWICK
BASEBALL'S PREEMINENT PIONEER
WRITER FOR HALF A CENTURY.
INVENTOR OF THE BOX SCORE,
AUTHOR OF THE FIRST RULE-BOOK
IN 1858. CHAIRMAN OF RULES
COMMITTEE IN FIRST NATION-WIDE
BASEBALL ORGANIZATION.

Henry Chadwick

Brooklyn and Baseball slowly faded into oblivion for the rest of the decade and barely showed a pulse. It wasn't until 1883 that it began a renaissance, and this is the point where our story on the birth of the team that eventually became the Dodgers begins. These were the men that started it all. They were the "The Boys of Spring."

CHAPTER ONE

A Team Grows in

Brooklyn

The story that comes down to us from the 1880s on the start of the team known as the Dodgers sees credit to a Newspaperman named George J. Taylor. He was the City Editor of James Gordon Bennett's "New York Herald" Taylor was 30 years old and a graduate of St. Frances Xavier College at 30 West 16th Street in the Chelsea section of New York City. He devised an idea for a Baseball team in Brooklyn following the debacle of Baseball in Brooklyn, which was noted erstwhile. The New York Herald was in Herald Square, where the Macy's Thanksgiving Day Parade is currently held annually.

A doctor recommended Taylor to find a different profession that involved the great outdoors to replace his pressure-laden job. Perhaps he drank, gambled, or inhaled too much coffee for his good, causing the doctor's recommendation. All we know is that he was a chain smoker. We have no idea what other vices might be involved here, but jobs like this invariably led to these so-called "habits." We will never know the truth, but I think it suffices that the daily responsibility of getting everything precise for a major city newspaper was demanding, exacting and never-ending. It was probably nerve-wracking as well! Let's not forget that in May of 1883, the Brooklyn Bridge was opened, which meant population growth for Brooklyn and a new audience for Baseball. George Taylor's timing was propitious.

New York Herald on the right, Macy's on the left

From all sources, we read that Taylor found an "Angel" (backer) from nearby Wall Street for his new ballpark in Brooklyn. When apprised of the potential costs for setting up shop for the new ball field in Brooklyn, the "Angel" supposedly backed out. Nowhere can we find the name of this hypothetical "Angel" Apparently, Taylor found land available from the Litchfield Corporation. It was the land eventually used for the new ballpark.

Now, however, Taylor had a big problem! He had signed papers to lease land from the Litchfield Corporation but now had no money to continue. Taylor needed a lawyer! (We don't know precisely how long he took to find the backer and land, but most of 1882 seems likely).

CHAPTER TWO
Now Comes Brice

There is no real explanation of how George J. Taylor found a lawyer. We know that he initially or eventually found his way to the doorstep of an attorney named John Brice. The only thing known was that Brice was somewhere in New York City! The population of New York City in 1880 was 1,200,000, so finding anyone would be a daunting task even then. (Brooklyn was the third largest American city then, with 566,000 right behind second-place Philadelphia. In 1880, Brooklyn was still separate from New York City and did not join it until January 1, 1898).

Fortunately, we had directories back in 1883 to look up names. These were the equivalents of phone books with which we are familiar today. Today, however, the internet is causing phone books to land on the almost extinct list—these directories listed only one's address, profession, and name. Fortuitously, when one would look up the name of John Brice, there was a subsequent result. Both his home address and business address were listed. His home was adjacent to what would become the Lincoln Tunnel in New York City. The tunnel would eventually connect New York City to New Jersey. He lived in a neighborhood inauspiciously known as "Hell's Kitchen." His law firm's address was 317 Broadway at the corner of Broadway and Thomas Street (then Liberty Street) in New York City.

All sources, without exception, indicate that George J. Taylor found attorney John Brice sometime in the winter of 1882-1883. We probably can discount the winter period between Christmas and New Year as a time of merriment. For the most part, work saw replacement with jollity, so this meeting most likely occurred after Tuesday, January 2, 1883.

John Brice's law firm at the corner of Broadway and Thomas Street, New York City (left)

We can only imagine the initial meeting between Brice and Taylor, but it probably saw a very distraught George J. Taylor seeking help from John Brice. He wanted to extricate himself from his confusion regarding the "Angel" and back out of the deal. All Taylor could tell Brice was that the matter was still not resolved and that the backer had laid out funds for the lease. That much is known, but exactly how much money was laid out for the lease was never disclosed.

Unbeknownst to Taylor, the potential savior to all his perils was sitting at a desk a few feet from the meeting between Taylor and Brice. The new potential savior was one with the moniker of Charles H. Byrne. Byrne was a real estate broker from South Brooklyn who parenthetically rented a desk from Brice for his business.

Brice told Taylor to retrieve the lease papers and come back with them. While Taylor was completing his task, Brice discussed Taylor's circumstances with Byrne, who had an idea of how to start the business.

Byrne and Taylor met later and discussed and noted that they had much in common. Both were graduates of St. Frances Xavier college in the Chelsea area of New York City, and the element that Byrne had most in common with Taylor was that he had been a sports reporter at some point. It assuredly made it inevitable that they would become fast friends through their common interests.

Brice's Law firm was at 317 Broadway at the corner of Thomas Street (Liberty Street back then). The original building is no longer there though the twin of it still stands directly across the street to the right in the picture. A McDonald's is located there today.

CHAPTER THREE

Charles Byrne the Napoleon of Baseball

Charles Byrne was 39 years old when he met George Taylor at John Brice's office. He was smallish even for those times, measuring in at 5' 2". What he lacked in size, he made up for in both style and personality, according to the scribes at that time. He was said to have a shimmering black mustache and a quick sarcastic wit. Byrne was bright, talkative, articulate even-tempered, and believed in honor and fair play. Most said that he was persuasive and could easily win over people to his point of view with his unfailing and unassailable logic. Stylistically he was considered a flashy, colorful dresser. One illuminator wrote, "Charley Byrne would be immaculate if there were a frost in Hades." Byrne was an aficionado of New York Opera, his favorite being "La Boheme." Later, he took his ball players to the Opera to try and foster an appreciation of the finer arts.

The funniest story regarding Byrne was when he supposedly "set a record of straight away talking for 10 hours, at which time only the bartender was left!" He was reputed to always be around the trendiest and well-known. Nobody could find anyone who had anything bad to say about Ole Charlie! He was a very amusing character.

As soon as Charlie heard of the Taylor circumstances, he sauntered down seven blocks to 12 Ann Street to visit his brother-in-law Joseph J. Doyle and apprise him of the goings-on with George Taylor. Doyle was interested! He told Charlie to return to Brice's office and make the arrangements necessary to procure both Taylor and the land. The "angel" rather than be sued, let George Taylor have the lease in lieu of any potential legal action by Taylor. It became his 5% interest in the team in the long road. Without this initially unintended meeting with the element of Charles H. Byrne added, we would have no story to tell.

Charles H. Byrne

Byrne had two big tasks in front of him. First, he had to find players for the nascent team. The game at that time was both rough and rowdy. Byrne and Taylor were committed to raising the level of play to attract a higher class of fans. They placed ads for players in the New York Clipper. They sought out temperate-minded "men of intelligence and not corner-lot toughs who happen to possess some skill as a player but whose habits and ways make them unfit for thorough teamwork." Lastly, the club needed to join a league. In March 1883, Brooklyn was accepted into the minor-league Interstate Base Ball Association, connecting with teams located in smaller towns in Pennsylvania, New Jersey, and Delaware. In a short time, Byrne and his colleagues had given naissance to a ballpark, a team, and joined a professional league. A new era of Brooklyn Baseball was about to start.

Undoubtedly Byrne did the lion's share of the work after the club saw establishment. We know of Taylor and his vanishing "Angel" but nothing else about what other preliminary steps he might have taken in advance. As a city editor for the New York Herald, he had to be thorough, and no doubt would have had to do a fair amount of research ahead of time.

Doyle always deferred to Byrne and claimed he did everything in its entirety, so it is logical to assume that he did not contribute much more than money and the support one would give a brother-in-law. Co-Owner Gus Abell was always in Newport, Rhode Island, from Memorial Day until Labor Day running his "Clubhouse." It had the moniker "the Nautilus Club." We can only speculate who did what, where, and when, as there is no other evidence to add to the mix.

The new Brooklyn team played their first home game at Washington Park on May 12, 1883. This was two weeks before the opening of the Brooklyn Bridge. The minor-league game was against Trenton, which Brooklyn won and attracted more than 6,000 cranks (fans). That very same day, Byrne hired a young assistant, a ticket-taker who did various other jobs. His name was Charles H. Ebbets, and he would become an iconic figure in the history of the Brooklyn Base Ball club. (Baseball was two words back then)

Ebbets was a handyman, a "jack of all trades" that filled in where needed. He claimed to oversee all the employees at the Park, looked after ticket sales, and purportedly printed up programs at some point. Ebbets described Byrne as a brilliant and forceful writer not only of letters but of newspaper articles and sporting sheets under various aliases. He had pen names to boost Brooklyn and exalt its position in the national sport, as seen in the Brooklyn Eagle on January 18, 1913, on page 23, written by none other than Charles Ebbets himself.

The "Brooklyn's," as they were called (not the Grays or Atlantics as is sometimes written), were known as the Polka Dots (because of their socks, no less!). It saw the light in a series of articles by Charles Ebbets from early January to March 11 of 1913 in the Brooklyn Eagle. The "polka dots" were middle-of-the-pack dwellers when the first-place Camden, New Jersey Merritt's disbanded. Byrne swiftly made a move that would become his trademark (with Gus Abell's money). Byrne, always the raconteur, was targeting a quick exit from the minor leagues into the big leagues. He seized the opportunity and targeted Camden's best players at top dollar with higher salaries. With the influx of the new Camden players, Byrne's team won the Interstate Association pennant. This was in the club's first year of existence.

In 1884, Byrne was able to talk his way into the American Association. The league was considered a major league along with the National League. The team, with co-founder George J.

Taylor as Manager, was a financial success but finished way down in the standings upon entering the American Association. They needed better players for the big leagues. But as 1885 began, Charles H. Byrne seemed to be doing naught. Suddenly news broke that at 1 AM on January 5, 1885, Brooklyn had signed the top players from the National League's Cleveland club, which had just been disbanded. Under Baseball guidelines, there was a ten-day waiting period before any team could sign any released players. Coincidentally or purposely, Byrne had hidden the players in a Cleveland hotel until the deadline passed. Once again, with co-owner Gus Abell bankrolling the purchase, Byrne struck with his "legere de main."

The other magnates were furious, but it made no difference. "The outraged and outwitted delegates from elsewhere discussed Messrs. Byrne and Abell in a manner that made the swearing of the army in Flanders sound like a Sunday school address – that was good it did them," said Charles H. Ebbets (In his History of Brooklyn Baseball published in the Brooklyn Eagle) The New York Times called the surprising signing "the biggest sensation ever made in Baseball." Brooklyn also signed the Cleveland manager. This required George Taylor to move to the front office as club secretary. Taylor returned to the newspaper business in 1885 after two years and was the first original owner to leave.

Also, in 1885 Brooklyn almost made it into the National League but would have to wait until 1890. The Providence, Rhode Island team retired from the National League, and the Brooklyn club endeavored to purchase the entire team and its' position in the National League for $10,000. When it came time to close the deal, it turned out that Providence had sold two players (Radbourn and Dailey) to Boston and could not include them in the agreement as initially constructed. Brooklyn pulled the deal off the table and could not enter the National League.

Charles H. Byrne became a field manager but failed to match his prowess in the front office. After losing the 1887 season, Byrne fired himself and, in his place, hired Baseball pioneer Bill "Gunner" McGunnigle as the club's Manager for the 1888 season.

Byrne next pulled off a historic deal with Chris Von der Ahe, St. Louis owner. He acquired three St. Louis stars for a record price of $19,000. The players were catcher Doc Bushong, outfielder Dave Foutz, and pitcher "Parisian Bob" Caruthers, who also signed a contract for a record payment of $5,500. According to many sources, Von der Ahe was strange and required three deals with three separate checks. Nobody knew why. The spectacular deal completed by Byrne made him the talk of the Baseball world. "Certainly, if pluck and energy, combined with a liberal outlay of money, can achieve success in securing first-class players with which to improve his team, Charley is going to get it." This was according to legendary Baseball Hall of Famer sports scribe Henry Chadwick.

Before the start of the 1888 season, five Brooklyn players got married, prompting Baseball raconteurs to give the team the appellation "The Bridegrooms." They were seemingly left at the altar that year, finishing second behind St. Louis. Charles H. Byrne was resolute. He unlocked Gus Abell's treasure chest to acquire star outfielders Pop Corkhill, Oyster Burns, second baseman Hub Collins, and pitcher Tom Lovett.

In 1889, Brooklyn battled St. Louis until the season's final day. After winning the final game in Columbus, Ohio, Charles H. Byrne and his Bridegrooms headed home by train, not knowing the result of the St. Louis match. When the train arrived, the team caught wind of the fact that St. Louis had lost, giving Brooklyn its first pennant. When Byrne heard the news, "his worried face relaxed into a contented smile, and his entire nervous system underwent a change," Sporting Life said. "The strain had been long and severe, and the reaction was immediate."

Byrne's comfort was that all his ploys to draw the average cranks to Brooklyn games resulted in a regular-season attendance of 336,000, the highest for any Baseball club in the 19th century.

CHAPTER FOUR

Joseph J. Doyle
Proprietor of 12 Ann St.

Charles Byrne's sister Cornelia was married to Joe Doyle. Where Byrne was heading on his seven-block stroll after hearing the Taylor story was one of the better-known gambling joints in New York City at the time, located at 12 Ann Street. One of at least a dozen such gaming lairs found on this street from 1850 to 1895.

The gambling craze arrived in New York City after the Civil War, and the games of choice were roulette and faro. Faro was a card game coming the last century from France. It traveled to New Orleans and up the Mississippi on Riverboats and into the lawless towns of the Old West. It's not too surprising that it also found its way into the "gilded age" during and after the time of the notorious Boss Tweed of Tammany Hall infamy.

1883 marked the year the Brooklyn Bridge opened so that access to Brooklyn became more accessible from Manhattan, and the population of Brooklyn was about to explode because of it. Doyle's gambling establishment saw location just south of the Manhattan exit of the soon-to-be-opened Brooklyn Bridge on Ann Street, a narrow one-way street three blocks long. Ann

Street was near Wall Street and is in the shadows of the recently built Freedom Tower that replaced the World Trade Center after its untimely demise. Ann Street is one of the oldest streets in New York City, first appearing on a map created in 1728. It was named after Ann White, the wife of merchant and developer Thomas White.

P.T. Barnum's Museum was located at the corner of Broadway and Ann Street in Manhattan from 1841 to 1865. On July 13, 1865, one of New York City's most famous (and morally questionable) museums burned to the ground. Doyle, while wealthy, could not swallow this undertaking all by himself. He had to find someone else who would join the new enterprise. It seems that these gambling joints were owned, co-owned, shared, managed, or divided in some manner. How the machinations of all this worked will never be gleaned since there could be no legal papers for illegal businesses. Of course, there is no one left to question.

Be that as it may, we know from newspaper articles that Joseph J Doyle was also associated with another gambling den, perhaps the most notorious of all, the "Central Club" located at 818 Broadway. Its owners included bookies Davy Johnson and Luce Appleby, who took bets on horses at places like Saratoga, New York. They were also related to gambling dens at Narragansett Pier and Newport in Rhode Island, though we will never know to what extent.

Ann Street today, which is 3 blocks long, very narrow, and built-in pre-automobile times

Barnum's Museum was located at the corner of Ann Street and Broadway

Suffice to say that any legal transaction had to be recorded in some sort of newspaper. It is where they dropped the sparse clues. All these clues needed to be woven together to put together a story. These folks never gave interviews to enlighten us further. They could be convicted of a crime by quoting their answers if they did.

Joseph J. Doyle was among those listed in a group that owned 818 Broadway, but the big name here was Ferdinand Augustus (Gus) Abell, the wealthiest gambler in all of New York City at the time. It was here that the fate of the ball team would lay, and it was here too also that Byrne and Doyle went.

27

Apparently typical was a paying 20% of the admitted profits to police and or politicians by the gambling hall owners. Sometimes it worked, other times not. In one story, we see the police attempting to break into 12 Ann St. but, failing to do so, broke into 13 Ann St. instead, assuming some connection. The owners of 13 Ann St. sued the police and won! Typical was paying 20% of the admitted profits to police or politicians by the gambling hall owners.

CHAPTER FIVE
Ferdinand Augustus (Gus) Abell

Gus Abell was an enigma. Considering the type of business he was in, it should be no great surprise. If you try to find him historically, be prepared to look under various appellations like Able and Abel and one not so obvious, Henry Morrison! There were also various first name permutations and combinations from F. Augustus, F.A., F., Frederick, or Gus.

Abell was born June 8, 1833, in Pawtucket, Rhode Island, to Robert Abell and Asenath Pearce Staples. His uncle was Arunah S. Abell, who founded the "Baltimore Sun" newspaper. We see an unremarkable youth other than the passing of his father when Gus was fifteen. Census and directory records show nothing notable except an address at 657 Providence Road in the 1850s. It wasn't until we got to 1860 and 1861, when Gus Abell was in his late twenties, that in the Providence, Rhode Island directories, we see associated with his name (F. A. Abel) "Clubhouse" (aka gambling joint) at 35 Weybosset Street.

Gus Abell sees a listing at his 21 West 37th street address in the Manhattan directory as a "Broker." (of what we have no clue-perhaps he helped people go broke?) We lose track of Gus until we see two New York addresses at 21 West 37th Street and 1 Ann Street in the mid-1860s. The last address was the location of a "Clubhouse" run by Jim Morrisey, notoriously the biggest name in New York Gambling after the Civil War and at the time visited by none other than Boss Tweed and his brother. Morrisey took Gus under his wing and tutored him. Here we probably got the name "Morrison" as having no father, Gus Abell became Morrisey's son hence "Morrison."

In December 1867 (from the New York Times), we see Abell and his then partner Albert M. Stokes involved in a lawsuit with Charles G. Patterson over money lost at the 1 Ann Street gambling club, one of many located on this street over that time.

In September of 1877, we note that the "Central Club" 818 Broadway was raided, and the gambling house closed. Mr. Henry Morrison, along with four others, were arrested. The police seized all the equipment.

In January of 1880, officer Sidney W. Conklin of the Society for the Suppression of Vice testified he was instructed to go into 818 Broadway and gather evidence about gambling at this location. He identified Abell as being Henry Morrison. When Abell testified, he asserted that he knew nothing about 818 Broadway or what went on there. Abell also added that he had no idea who Henry Morrison was. Abell was released on his own recognizance.

Early in 1883, Joseph J. Doyle, an associate of Gus Abell's, came to him with his brother-in-law Charles H. Byrne with the idea of starting a Baseball team in Brooklyn. Abell was told the idea came from George J. Taylor, the City Editor of James Gordon Bennett's New York Herald. Abell knew all about Bennett since Abell had recently started a "Society Club" on

30

Bath Road in Newport, Rhode Island, right behind a casino built by Bennett. This was the club that eventually became known as the Dodgers.

FERDINAND A. ABELL

Abell's "Nautilus Club" in Newport, Rhode Island, at the turn of the century

Abell's Clubhouse, also known as the "Nautilus Club," is the Canfield House today (note hidden back door on left). Canfield was an employee of Gus Abell's at 818 Broadway and learned his trade from him. When Abell wanted to sell the gambling, joint Canfield bought it from him in 1899 through Abell left Newport in 1897.

The fine detail of the interior can still be seen today. The same could have been said of 818 Broadway. 1880's styling is in evidence.

On February 12, 1873, Gus Abell and William H. Mc Kee bought a small house (7 Bath Street) still located to the left of the Canfield House for $7500. (Though the street is now called Memorial Blvd.) Three years later, in 1876, they bought the land (9 Bath Street) that is the Canfield house today for $11,250. Directories at the time show Abell on Catharine Avenue in Newport until 1874. By the time the Casino was built and opened by Bennett in 1880, Abell's gambling establishment was working at full bore. The Tennis Hall of fame is located there, and many a critical tennis match has been held on these hallowed grounds, plus a glorious celebration of the History of Tennis itself.

James Gordon Bennett's award-winning Casino then and now.

In July of 1886, we find a truthful expose about Abell and Doyle and all their friends and gambling associates in Cincinnati and St. Louis. For some reason, these stories never filtered their way back east to New York. This is odd given the press' propensity to follow a lead down any conceivable wormhole. Let's not forget Gus Abell's good friend James Gordon Bennett of New York Herald fame. Did he quash the story for Abell? We can only speculate.

On August 2, 1888, we saw that Mayor Powell of Newport told Gus Abell and his partner William H. McKee not to open their gambling joint, but that seems to have just faded away with nothing happening as eight years later, we read from the New York World of June 1896, "F. A. Abell stands high in the opinion of the frequenters of his cottage. He has, it is said, some civic connection with the city of Newport. One's first impression of Abell is that he is a gentleman, courteous, accomplished, and high-bred. It is said that he is of good birth and came from Mexico. Whatever his origin, he is certainly an interesting character. Does it occur to the patrons of this gaming cottage that the proprietor's habits are very superior to their own? A real gambler rarely drinks, for example. His hands and nerves must be steady. For this reason, also his health is a matter of first consequence. Abell seldom drinks, and his health is the envy of many persons." It is also said that he was always dressed impeccably and was very well-groomed.

Both 818 Broadway (the "Central Club") and his "Clubhouse" in Newport were always labeled as having an indescribable air of comfort. They were luxuriously laid out with expensive, finely oiled wood, emphasizing the colors of red and gold, with high Cathedral ceilings adorned with the most delicate crystal chandeliers. They both had the finest food from the best chefs' bar none. Even the Vanderbilt's said as much.

There is psychology here in that the circumstances gamblers were in are of the most primal feelings of fight or flight. There was much at risk. If the marks were uncomfortable, they might leave. An air of first-class high culture and luxury was set to allay their natural flight tendencies. It also made them more amenable to being fleeced. America and its puritanical heritage are no better seen as in the Massachusetts and Rhode Island of this time. Nowhere did we find the feeling of permissiveness that permeated the air in Monte Carlo anywhere in this world. (Hence the hidden back entrance to Abell's Clubhouse)

The Rear Entrance to Abell's.

(From a photograph taken for the Sunday World.)

Those who do not care to be seen entering Abell's from fashionable Bath road enter down Bellevue avenue and through this gate. The gate is to Abell's what side doors are to saloons.

American Royalty with notables like Vanderbilt, Havemeyer, Beach, Hoyt, Buckley, Van Alen, Brice, and Goelet found their way to Abell's side door. However, none would admit it or even consider using the front door. Gambling was a toy of the wealthy, just as Newport was at that time. It was, after all, Mark Twain's monikered "Gilded Age" with all the feelings, mannerisms, amenities, accouterments, and decorative adjectives and adverbs so vividly described by F. Scott Fitzgerald in his "The Great Gatsby." (Though historically, Gatsby was slightly later). We can almost feel the presence of a Meyer Wolfsheim type permeating the air there somewhere as well. Many who did not play golf were decked out in golf finery just for its' association with money.

In 1883, with his name being used and three recent charges and arrests in New York City, Gus Abell was reluctant to back the team that later became known as the Dodgers. He had to remain hidden along with his fellow crony Joseph J. Doyle of 12 Ann Street fame. There were Puritans in New York as well, it seems.

If you remember L, Frank Baum's novel from whence the movie the "Wizard of Oz" sprang with Professor Marvel (the wizard) being exposed by Toto pulling back the curtain, Gus Abell wanted no reprise of that scene, so he had to create his own hidden "Wizard." Hence, Charles H. Byrne became the team's figurehead, orator, and president and was marched out for public consumption whenever needed (even though he only owned about 5% of the team). For a decade, the only place we saw Abell's name was when a legal announcement had to be made requiring the placement of a notice in a newspaper. So, hidden in the back of the Brooklyn Eagle on Saturday, March 10, 1883, we see a small ad buried amongst ads for used baby carriages and broken glass that no one would be looking for. In that ad, we see the full lineup of the true owners for the first and last time in the 1880s.

Amongst them was a woman named Annie Taylor (who was the idea man George J. Taylor's wife). She had four shares but was conspicuously left out. When Abell finally sold 818 Broadway on July 12, 1890, we find his name now associated with Baseball for the first time. He no longer had to fear retribution in New York. As far as Rhode Island was concerned, it was rumored that he was associated with a "social club" at Narragansett Pier. One of his partners at the "Central Club" 818 Broadway was Davy Johnson (a bookie associated with horse racing and Saratoga), who seems to have run that location. Gus Abell was strictly in Newport.

We will never honestly know the answer to that, as gamblers kept no records from which we can glean information. No records of any real estate holdings can be found in any public records. Another rumor was that Abell had businesses in the northeast and property holdings in New York City. These were mere contrivances to protect Abell and give an air of preeminence, invisibility, and power. Sell the sizzle, not the steak, so to speak. This ruse did not have to last forever because, in 1883, Gus Abell was already 50.

The most amusing story Abell used to tell was that he owned a farm in Newport, Rhode Island. It was an inside joke understood by a few. Perhaps he was correct. The only difference is that he farmed gamblers, not vegetables! Abell's web of intrigue was both deep and profound.

Slowly but surely, Abell needed to extricate himself from his web or be consumed by it as he grew into old age. As mentioned, in 1890, he sold his 818 Broadway club as gambling in New York was moving further north near Times Square.

In 1894, Gus Abell purchased a Villa in West Yarmouth near Main Street (now Route 28) and Berry Avenue (The Town & Country Motor Lodge is currently located there). The only hint we have of the land's former usage is located one block north of the intersection of Berry Avenue and route 28 near a CVS store. It is a road appropriately named "Abell's Road."

He spent at least his last 15 years there. In 1898, after the death of his long-time friend Charles H. Byrne he sold his shares in the Brooklyn Team to Charles H. Ebbets of Ebbets Field claim (even though they weren't fully cashed out until 1907, according to all sources). In 1894, after his partner in "The Nautilus Club," aka "the Clubhouse," William H. McKee died, we find legal proceedings being brought against Abell by McKee's widow Mary Cora Mc Kee. A public auction was held in 1895 when Abell purchased the "Clubhouse" and bought out the dowager for $35,000. Two years later, we see his name removed from the Newport directory of 1897.

His Clubhouse was sold in 1899 to Richard A. (Dick) Canfield, who cut his teeth as a dealer at Abell's 818 Broadway, aka the "Central Club." The selling price was $65,000. Canfield became an even more successful gambler than Abell and was given the "Prince of Gambling" moniker. Today's house is known as the "Canfield House"; nobody, including the Historical Association, knew about Abell. He kept his secrets all too well, which he probably wanted to do anyway.

The last piece fell into place when Abell sold his mansion in New York City at 22 West 42nd Street between Madison and Fifth Avenues to the Manhattan Hotel in 1899. He was now free to peacefully pursue the remaining fourteen years of his life in the quaint Cape Cod Town of West Yarmouth just east of Hyannis. Gus passed away on November 8, 1913, at the age of 80 of Bright's Disease, from a kidney disease known as Nephritis. It was the same thing his buddy Charles H. Byrne died from. His wife, Almira, died in 1908. Gus and Almira had no children, and all his siblings predeceased him. A niece and nephew inherited the bulk of his estate. Gus and Almira are buried in Swan Point Cemetery on the Seekonk River that feeds into the Providence River just south of where Gus was born in Pawtucket.

Abell's West Yarmouth, Massachusetts Villa, located on affluent Cape Cod, has since been razed and is now the Town and Country Motor Lodge. It is situated near Abell's road. The only sign left today that he ever was even there

CHAPTER SIX

The Birth of the Dodgers

The Brooklyn Base Ball Club became a legal entity on Friday, March 9, 1883, at 10:14 AM. How can we say that? It says so on the Certificate of Association effected by John Brice and duly executed at the Brooklyn County Clerk's Office that same day. It took March 7th and 8th to complete and sign all the documents. The papers weren't legal until duly executed on March 9 and filed at the county clerk's office on Court Street.

**Copy of part of Certificate of Association showing shares—
below is the breakdown.**

Breakdown of Ownership

Owner's Name	# of shares	% Percentage of Ownership	Dollar Amount laid out
Ferdinand (Gus) Augustus Abell	2411	81%	$16226
Joseph J. Doyle	242	8%	$1629
Charles H. Byrne	154	5.25%	$1037
George D. Taylor	154	5.25%	$1037
John Brice	4	1.2%	$27
Annie Taylor	4	1.2%	$27
John M. Kelly	4	1.2%	$27

We can see that $20,000 was laid out to capitalize the team. Gus Abell owned 81% of the team and laid out 81% of the money. Joe Doyle laid out 8%. The tandem of Charles Byrne and George Taylor owned 5.25% each.

Where the money for Charles Byrne's shares came from can only be speculated upon. He was not a man of means. It might have come from his brother-in-law Joseph J. Doyle as a gift due to familial connections (Doyle was married to Byrne's sister Cornelia) and because Byrne needed to become the figurehead of the operation to protect Abell. (as per next chapter). It seems logical that Taylor brought the land and its lease to the table and is the source of his shares. Annie Taylor was George's wife and probably did some work that earned her 4 shares.

The last two owners were John Brice and John M. Kelly. Brice's shares perhaps were in lieu of his legal fees. It was thought impossible to figure out who John M. Kelly was, given the formidable number of Irishmen with the last name of Kelly in New York City.

Nevertheless, a search of all the period directories was done to see if a glimmer of who he was could be found. The only scant clue garnered was the middle initial "M." The next logical strategy was the listed professions of all the John M. Kelly's recorded in the New York City Directories.

In the end, only one listing in any period directory made sense. There was a John M. Kelly listed as a broker. His shares must have come from the commission he would have received in the real estate deal. He possibly took shares in lieu of a commission. He must have been George Taylor's real estate connection regarding the "Angel" who backed out of the initial deal that prompted Taylor to seek out Brice initially.

Brooklyn Base Ball Association.

The Brooklyn Base Ball Association have filed certificate of association in the County Clerk's office. The capital named is $20,000, and the directors Ferdinand A. Abell, Joseph J. Doyle, Charles H. Byrne, George D. Taylor and John M. Kelley. The grounds are between Fourth and Fifth avenues, Third and Fourth streets, with entrance on Fifth avenue.

Real Owners showed for the first time hidden in reader ads.

When a corporation is started, it is legally required to place an announcement in the newspapers of the event. It is at that moment we perceive who the real owners are. If one looks closely at the notice which was found on the last page of the Brooklyn Eagle on March 9, 1883 (the same date the Corporation was started), one finds the above-publicized notice. It was located amongst reader ads for various used things, including castoff furniture and gently used clothing, and other various and sundry hand-me-down items. No one knew of the new club and its ownership, so only a very astute eye would pick up on the ad's true meaning. In fact, it was only about a decade later that the true ownership was revealed. It is precisely the obscurity, the new ownership wanted.

THE BROOKLYN CLUB

was incorporated last week under the title of the Brooklyn Baseball Association, with Charles H. Byrne of Brooklyn as its president, and George Taylor of Brooklyn as secretary and manager, and with a paid-up capital of $20,000, nearly $14,000 of which will have been expended before the first championship game is played on its ground in May next. The work of preparing the new grounds in erecting the fence to inclose it was begun on March 5, and it is work which involves a greater outlay than was at first anticipated, inasmuch as it is necessary to dump about 10,000 cubic yards of earth along the sides of the field, which is 600ft. long by 450ft. wide, so as to secure a good foundation for the fences. As fast as this work progresses that of erecting the fences, building the grand and open stands and the other necessary structures will be pushed forward, so that the ground will be ready for play about the middle of April.

New York Clipper March 10, 1883, page 818 shows only Byrne and Taylor as owners.

Beginning immediately and as seen above, we perceive only the names of Charles H. Byrne and George Taylor listed for public consumption. There was a reason for this which will be delved into in the next chapter. Also, note that the work on the new grounds was begun on March 5, 1883, which is verified by a second source, that being the March 5, 1883, issue of Brooklyn Union Newspaper, stating that the work was started that day.

This is important because other historical sources claim different time frames for the date the earth was moved initially.

What makes sense is that all this transpired in two months, from January 2, 1883, to March 9, 1883. All other stories found could not also fit into this same time frame. Of course, having the original Certificate of Association in hand and some backup verifiable news sources as proof authenticate the original start date and the owners' names. The reasons for all this obfuscation and mystification will be graphically explained in the next chapter.

CHAPTER SEVEN

Babel Redux

The first question here is, why all the mystery and drama? The answer comes from what happened in the prior decade. From the March 31, 1883 issue of the Brooklyn Eagle, we read: "The Baseball public of our great cities have never lost their admiration of the national game itself, but years ago, in the Baseball centers of New York and Philadelphia, the patrons of the game became disgusted with the then-existing rottenness of the professional fraternity at large, and they determined to put a stop to it by keeping away from the public ball grounds, and this they did until after the time that professional play had reached its lowest ebb in public estimation, and had almost died of the cancer of "crookedness. "Then came an era of quietness in Baseball in both cities, as far as professionalism was concerned, during which period the expulsion of the worst class of "crooks" from the principal clubs and the successful opposition presented to the kindred evil of pool gambling in connection with professional club business." The article further claimed that "honest play has been revived, the old-time love of the game was developed again with all its honest play was the fundamental principle of the new association and this it was which led to the great pecuniary success attendant upon the American Association's first season."

Gambling had been problematic, and these new squires in Brooklyn had promised to be gentlemen and fair in their dealings in the rebirth of Base Ball in Brooklyn and not be part of past problems. They had a big problem in that regard. All the money that started the team came from gambling profits, and to be successful, they had to hide that fact or face failure.

The first thing done was to create an Oz-like figurehead. In that regard, Charles H. Byrne was paraded out as their squeaky clean "wizard" of goodness and virtue. He had a spotless record. Of course, George J. Taylor also had a sparkling record and supposedly came up with the idea for the team from the start. Taylor was also their original Manager. Curiously though, he managed for approximately the team's first two seasons and was gone. In 1885, Taylor returned to the journalism field; he left because of bad health caused by the stress of the journalism field. The truth of why he went back will never be known. He faded into obscurity. We see him listed as a lawyer in a 1910 New York City directory. One year later, he died at age 59 on October 28, 1911, and is buried in the same Calvary cemetery that Charles Byrne was buried in. (Taylor was born November 22, 1852)

So, where is the smoking gun? On Friday, January 23, 1880, in the Newport Daily News, on page two, we get the first inkling of "F. A. Abell owns a place on Bath Road and has been arrested for keeping a gambling house in New York." If you recall the previous chapter on Abell, you will understand how deep Abell's gambling roots went. Three years later, when the team was at its birthing, this is something that could not be revealed, particularly in light of what happened to Brooklyn Baseball in the 1870s. Hence cover stories had to be fashioned. The problem was that while these stories were created, they weren't remembered exactly and changed as the years went by due to faulty memories and lousy reporting. They all knew the truth but forgot the lies creating various versions that have been quoted as fact but never agreed to when one compares the stories. The best you can get is that the information appeared to be ambiguous.

In the Brooklyn Eagle of January 4, 1898, we read that, 14 years earlier, in 1885, Mr. Taylor retired, and Mr. Byrne, Doyle, and Abell incorporated, changing their name from Byrne, Doyle, and Company. This belies the fact that there already was a corporation. All that had to be done was buy Taylor's 5 % of the stock.

On January 18, 1913 (30 years after the fact), on page 23 of the Brooklyn Eagle, we read that Doyle laid out $12,000 to prepare the land. The last chapter disproves this. They began land preparation on March 5, 1883, and the Corporation paid for it. The same source claims that it took Doyle a long time to convince Abell to join. The last chapter shows everything that happened in 60 days, so where is a long time?

In the New York Clipper of March 4, 1898, 15 years after the fact, it was claimed that John Brice drew up co-partnership papers for Taylor, Byrne, and Doyle. After spending $12,000 on the land, they found Abell, which again is disproved by the evidence in the last chapter that it was a corporation from day one.

On the cover of the Sporting News on January 7, 1899, it was claimed that Abell did not join until the team was in the American Association. Again, this is not in agreement with the legal papers.

When Charles H. Byrne died, we find in his obituaries that in both the Sporting News and the New York Times that it was claimed Abell did not join the group until after the team was in the American Association. The Sporting News went further and said Doyle didn't participate until the club was in the American Association. The original certificate of association clearly shows Gus Abell as the chief owner from day one on March 9, 1883, with Doyle there.

In Frank Graham's book on the Brooklyn Dodgers from 1945, on page four, it claims that Taylor just went to his three friends with the deal and that an R. I. Byrne was the last to join. Nowhere other than in Graham's book do we find any reference to an R. I. Byrne. No R. I. Byrne can be found anywhere, so historically where that name came from is unknown. At the reading of Byrnes' will in 1898, we see his brother William G. Byrne in attendance along with his sister Cornelia who was the wife of Joseph J. Doyle.

As one can see, this is a dilemma of significant proportions. Notice that all these references were 15 years on or later than when they happened. All these supposed partnerships, co-partnerships, and groupings never included the name of Abell. There was a time when this changed, and the event that changed it was when Gus Abell sold his gambling house at 818 Broadway in New York City, as seen below.

"EIGHT-EIGHTEEN" IS NO MORE.

THE LAST DAYS OF A ONCE FAMOUS GAMBLING RESORT.

For thirty years or more the heavy blinds on the quiet, old-fashioned house at 818 Broadway have been kept religiously closed. The place presented such a wonderfully sedate appearance, surrounded as it is by busy mercantile establishments, that people who did not know its true character were attracted to it by its very quietness.

For thirty years or more this house has been known to men about town who longed occasionally for relaxation simply as "No. 818," and within its walls hundreds of thousands, perhaps millions, of dollars have changed hands, for 818 has been in its time one of the best-known and most liberally-patronized gambling houses in America.

Joe Hall, who just before, during, and for a time after the civil war was known as the "King Gambler" of New-York, started the place in 1859, when Union Square was almost a suburb, and it straightway became a resort of wondrous popularity.

For a time the glittering John Morrissey had practical control of 818, and in his reign—a reign contemporaneous with that of the amiable Tweed—play was heaviest there. The politicians who bled the city were wont to repair to Morrissey's place and forget their consciences in the excitement of gambling.

Within the last fifteen years 818 has been in many hands, and latterly it has rapidly gone to pieces. It got to be too far down town, and places of business crowded it too much for the comfort of its patrons. So its managers, Appleby & Abel, determined to close it up. They have removed all the furniture, gambling apparatus, &c., from the building, have given up business there, and in a short time old 818 will be turned into a place of business.

We finally see Gus Abell actively taking a more visible role in the club. He didn't have anything left to lose as the police and his 818 Broadway "Clubhouse," aka the "Central Club," could no longer hurt him or his reputation. Abell still had the Nautilus club in Newport, Rhode Island. Still, he misdirected people with a rumor about a club on Narragansett pier, run by one of his former partners at 818 Broadway named Davy Johnson, who we can find reference to in the Brooklyn Standard Union from Friday, June 30, 1911, page 11. We still see historical references to Narragansett Pier in Frank Graham's book of 1945 entitled "The Brooklyn Dodgers an Informal History" and an article from the Brooklyn Citizen dated Friday, December 11, 1936, on page 40.

The whole point was to obfuscate and misdirect with as much misinformation and disinformation as possible. This all happened in an era where news did not travel very fast or, in some cases, not at all. In that regard, we see an article from the Cincinnati Enquirer from Friday, July 16, 1886. The same article was repeated the next day in the St. Louis Post Dispatch. The club was only three years old then, and the story blew the entire cover story about Abell and Doyle wide open. It was also correct. Somehow it never made it back to the New York Papers!

Perhaps James Gordon Bennett and his New York Herald helped repress the story. After all, he and Abell had a solid connection in Newport, Rhode Island, as seen in the Chapter on Gus Abell in this book.

Confusion and Illusion were operatives here; we're both willful and purposeful. Researchers have played it safe for decades and quoted the quotes without any real insight. Even today, it is challenging to dig out the true story. Here Babel has finally been climbed and decoded.

It was quite an exhausting process to try and finally make sense of all this contradictory information. It was the stuff of an English drawing-room drama.

CHAPTER EIGHT
Washington Park 1

The team was known originally as just the "Brooklyn's." There were some references to the nickname "polka-dots" due to their socks. They leased land from the Litchfield Corporation on Fifth Avenue in Brooklyn to build Washington Park 1, the team's original home. Why choose the name Washington Park? Historically, this area was the site of the Battle of Brooklyn (aka Battle of Brooklyn Heights or Battle of Long Island), fought bravely by George Washington during the Revolutionary War for independence from Great Britain. It is also right near the Gowanus Canal, whose unforgettable smells still waft through the memories of my mind when I was a youth in the area. Many articles have claimed that the Park was either in the Red Hook or Park Slope area of Brooklyn. It was in the Gowanus section of Brooklyn. A real slick interpretation claims that the Park was between Red Hook and Park Slope, which is accurate and neatly skirts using the Gowanus name. It is obfuscation at its very best.

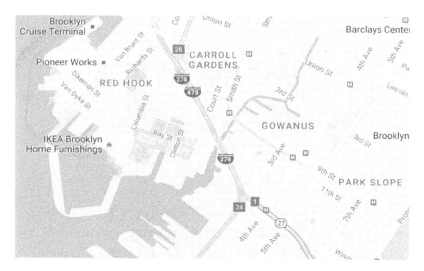

Red hook is on the left, Park Slope on the right. The field was located slightly above and right of Gowanus.

Gowanus was named after a Canarsie Indian chief named Gowanee, "the dreamer." No one wanted to admit to the name Gowanus because of the nearby Gowanus Canal.

Brooklyn comes from the Dutch name "Breukelen," which means broken land. It can best be explained geologically by the fact that Brooklyn, Queens, and all of Long Island are a terminal moraine of the Pleistocene Epoch. Rocks and dirt were pushed down from Canada and New England and deposited exactly where Long Island is located as the ice retreated north. Hence the broken land moniker.

In recent times, Gowanus has been called the "Disneyland of Pollution," as soon as the Industrial Revolution began, it became a depository of all detritus and debris. Today, EPA Superfund money has been used to remove 11 feet of what is referred to as "Black Mayonnaise" along with wagon wheels, tires, rusted cars, and old ice boxes, among a myriad of other dilapidated treasures. The mob used the canal as a depository for their dead bodies. The infamous Al Capone got his start here before being shipped to Chicago by Frankie Yale to wreck his nefarious calling on the poor denizens of that unfortunate Midwest city.

Gowanus Canal is seen today with Gowanus Expressway in the background.

Part of the team's property included the historical "Vechte" house seen below where George Washington's troops were located. It later served as the Dodgers clubhouse from 1884 until they moved in 1891. It is now a historic site called "The Old Stone House."

Clais Vechte's house past and now

Note the multitude of people skating on "Washington Pond" The Vechte house was later to become the Dodger team clubhouse can be seen in the background top right.

Washington Park 1 1883 to 1891 is seen here.

The original Certificate of Association shows that the team started with $20,000 of capital and was formed under the New York State Act of 1861, entitled "Act to provide for the incorporation of Skating Parks and Sporting Grounds." In light of that, "Ice Baseball" on skates was a winter event held at Washington Park during that time. The Park's name was changed to Washington Pond for the winter months. Before that, it was called Litchfield Pond after its landowner. Before the ball field was built, a Washington Pond for winter skating existed at this location. The rules were like Baseball rules except for ten fielders and a supposed red Baseball being used (a white one extant). Skaters could overshoot each base while skating, and the game was limited to 5 innings. Bases were etched into the ice. Owners booked various events throughout the year as Base Ball was in its infancy and not a great income provider, so other sources of income had to be found. The first recorded game of ice Baseball took place on February 4, 1861, on Washington Pond between the Atlantics and Charter Oaks teams and was witnessed by 12,000 people. *The Brooklyn Eagle* reported the wonderful tone of the game and that only a few players slipped, but those did provide a "source of merriment."

The land lease from the Litchfield Corporation was for 10 years, so moving was already built-in as a definite possibility from inception. In its very first year, the team played in the minor-league Inter-State Association of Professional Clubs, winning the league championship. It might not have happened, but the league-leading Camden Merritt's from New Jersey folded in July. Using Abell's money, Byrne quickly snapped up the Merritt's five best players and predictably rushed to the League championship. Having attracted a following, Byrne negotiated his way into the American Association in 1884, just in time for the one-year Union Association player war. The American Association was a competitor to the more established National League, which Byrne also talked his way into in 1890, demonstrating the "wizardry" expected of him

The above woodcut by C. J. Taylor was from Harper's Magazine in 1884 when Washington Park first opened. (Note the Grandstands in the background were constructed one year earlier in 1883)

Two of the owners tried their hand as field managers as very little was known about managing a team at this early date anyway. George Taylor went 40-64 in 1884, and Charles Byrne went 174-172 from 1885-1887.

At midnight on Saturday, May 15th, 1889, while the club was on an extended western road trip, an amateur Baseball game was played at Washington Park 1 between the Crescent and Staten Island Athletic Baseball clubs. It is thought that maybe one of the players left a lit cigar after the game ended. By the early hours of the following day, the grandstand and a significant portion of the Fifth Street fence had totally burned to the ground. (according to the Brooklyn Eagle). It wasn't discovered until after it demolished the entire grandstand, much of which had just been rebuilt that spring. The blaze started and was never figured out, but no evidence was left that the amateur teams caused a nasty cigar inferno.

Anti-tobacco reformers, of course, claimed it was caused by a cigarette or cigar stump. The Sunday Observance League, not to be surpassed, said it was just retribution from a vengeful God because they did not keep holy the sabbath as they played Sunday ball games at the Ridgewood, Queens field. They could not do so at Washington Park 1 due to Sunday Blue Laws. The local Fire chief delivered his professional opinion that "some bonehead was careless with his matches." As per the Brooklyn Eagle, conspiracy theories abounded then as now to fill the airspace with endless hogwash. Sticking out above these theories was the salient fact that the grandstand had gone up in smoke, but the bleachers and the club offices were saved. At least, they didn't blame it on some supposed alien invasion from Clarion.

According to Minnie Ebbets (Charles's wife) in a New York Daily News article on September 28, 1941, "I remember the fire. Charlie ran into the office through the smoke. He came out with his eyebrows singed and his hair burned, but he had the books." "He was a good deal more than a bookkeeper rather a business manager for the club. He made out the players' contracts, paid them off, and superintended road trips, in addition to keeping books."

The loss was about $18,000, with $7,000 covered by insurance. Insurance adjusters and architects were on hand bright, and early on Sunday and the clearing away of the debris began on Monday, May 17, 1889, and a new Grandstand, "greater, grander and more gorgeous than ever, with every modern improvement, was created, (built of wood)," again as per the Brooklyn Eagle.

The Park was not like current concrete and steel parks and was mainly made from wood. Workers toiled day and night, and the new, larger grandstand was in place for a double header with the defending champion St. Louis team on May 30. This feat was accomplished in just 13 days!! No home games were missed. The Brooklyn Eagle also reported the grandstand was "built in the strangest manner and bolted so that it can be easily moved or carried away if necessary." It sat about 4,000. Brooklyn's deadly enemies, from St. Louis, were there on May 30, and they won the morning game by an 8 to 4 score before 8,642 cranks. In the afternoon, Brooklyn was cheered on to victory by 22,000 spectators, while 4,000 who could not enter stood around the gates with no available seats.

From some of the first Baseball Cigarette cards from the era (the 1887 Old Judge cards) included below, we can see how the grandstands looked and how poorly the grounds were tended. (Note the grass, for example.) Many colleges today have far better facilities than these early wooden ballparks.

On October 8, 1887, Charles H. Byrne, with Gus Abell's money, bought the entire Metropolitan base ball team. Byrne claimed that in the negotiations between John B. Day and Mr. Wiman, he offered Mr. Wiman $25,000 for the whole of the franchise lock, stock, and barrel. It was at once accepted.

(According to the Indianapolis Journal from October 9, 1887.) The real treasure in the deal was a 250-pound first baseman named Dave Orr. He was the only player to ever hit it over the rear wall in Washington Park 1, even beyond the cranks sitting in the outfield. He inspired the phrase "Knock it into the Gowanus Canal" The current-day New York Mets took their name from this historical Metropolitan team.

1887 Old Judge cards are from the author's Dodger Museum collection. Note poorly groomed grass at Washington Park 1 and the primitive Baseball glove as seen on either side.

Washington Park saw two additional pennants for the club. The first of these was a down-to-the-wire finish over rivals from St. Louis. It happened in the American Association in 1889.

On October 17, 1889, a challenge series between the American Association champion "Bridegrooms" and National League champion New York Giants saw agreement. The clubs' two owners, John B. Day of the New York Giants club and Charles H. Byrne of the Brooklyn club, met and arranged a post-season series. They had an agreement that the Series would end when one club achieved six wins. The Series started the next day and continued until October 29, when the Giants won their sixth game. Attendance was reasonably good for the first two games of the Series, at the Polo Grounds and Washington Park. The weather then became cold and rainy. The remainder of the Series was sparsely attended.

The Giants won the best-of-11-games Series, 6 games to 3. The 1889 challenge series was the first that only saw New York City area clubs. It became the first part of a long-standing tradition that developed between New York clubs, particularly the Giants and the Dodgers. The game became known as the mayor's trophy game later. Brooklyn was a separate city at this time. Brooklyn (and the other three boroughs) would later merge with New York City beginning in 1898.

The New York Yankees would not enter the fray until New York Knickerbocker Beer magnate Jake Rupert bought the team in 1913 and started infusing beer money into the team. Beer money equaled championships.

Despite these Series setbacks, the Brooklyn team returned strong in 1890. The club joined the National League, and with the Giants suffered raids by the Players' League. Regardless it would still win the league championship. They became the first major league club to win consecutive pennants in two different leagues.

They then celebrated their debut season in the National League in 1890, winning the National League crown. The sad story was the fate of their Manager William (Gunner) McGunnigle. The following year a merger was encouraged (forced) with the Players League by the National League magnates wherein the additional owners compelled that their Manager John Montgomery Ward would run the team. The "Bridegrooms" proprietors had to replace their successful and well-liked Manager William (Gunner) McGunnigle, who had just won two championships. These new additional owners also required a move to their home field in the Brownsville section of East New York. The Washington Park lease was ending in any event.

1890 National League Championship team, the Brooklyn Bridegrooms (Manager William "Gunner" Mc Gunnigle is in the middle)

After losing the 1889 challenge series to their "cross-town" rivals, the New York Giants (Brooklyn was a separate city until 1898), the Bridegrooms returned strong. They won the National League pennant in 1890. They were the first major league club to win consecutive pennants in two different leagues (the only other one being the Boston Reds (1890–1891).

The major league Baseball world was in turmoil in 1890, as many of the best players had jumped to an outlaw organization monikered the Players' League. Although the Brotherhood only lasted one season, it had a detrimental financial effect on the other two leagues, especially the American Association.

The Boston Reds of the Players' League were likely the best team in the major leagues, and they came up with the idea of a three-way World Series, but the established leagues ignored them. They made arrangements for the usual NL-AA contest, this time to be a conventional best-4-of-7 Series.

The competitions were held at the "Bridegrooms" home field, Washington Park, and the Colonels' home field, Eclipse Park. The first four games were played in Louisville (including a tie in Game 3). The remainder of the Series was scheduled to occur in Brooklyn.

The Series started on October 17 and concluded on October 28. The weather became progressively worse as the Series wore on, and before Game 7, the two managers agreed this would be the final game, and if Louisville won, it would square the Series at 3–3–1 (which they did). The Series ended because of disinterest, with no one winning or showing up.

There would no longer be any more major league games at Washington Park 1 after that season, as the "Bridegrooms" (who assumed that nickname due to the marriages of five of their players in 1888) merged with the Brooklyn Wonders. The latter had one year of existence in the brotherhood league in 1890. The lease on Washington Park finally lapsed at the end of 1892, and in April 1893, the city began grading work to even out the slope of the area and buried much of the park in 16 feet of dirt.

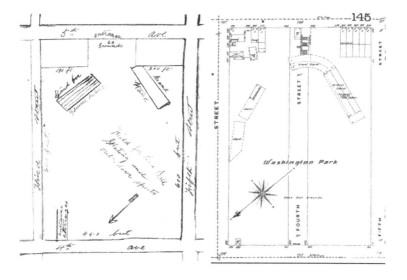

Field for Base Ball Skating and out-door sports - diagram of Washington Park 1 drawn by the Brooklyn Base Ball Club's founders in 1883 as seen from the original Certificate of Association (on left). Washington Park as seen 5 years later from the 1888 Sanborn map for comparison.

Site of Washington Park 1 in Brooklyn today. It is now called the J.J. Byrne Playground. These pictures were taken diagonally across the street from where Washington Park II would later be located. Photos were taken by the author.

CHAPTER NINE

The War with the Players League

The players league (or brotherhood league) was established by players disenchanted with labor relations in the existing organized baseball structure. The first such player's war happened in 1884, just as The Brooklyn team joined the American Association. It was called the Union Association war and lasted one year. The new Players League war offered teams in which the players retained partial ownership. The driving force behind it was a human dynamo known as John (Monte) Montgomery Ward, a baseball hall of famer, PGA player, and yes, a lawyer! After failing to change the one-sided player-management relationship, the notion of controlling their destiny and income attracted most of the game's stars, and the status of those stars cut profoundly into the existing professional leagues. Of the 72 players appearing in Players League box scores on April 19, only two had played in either the National League or American Association in 1889.

Monte Ward Ball Player, Lawyer, and Golf Pro

Brotherhood members (a players Union started in 1885) left their respective leagues and formed the Players' League. They had after failed to change the lopsided player-management relationship of the extant leagues. The league was started by the players. Fundamentally, it was an elaborate job action to advance their lot. However, the endeavor proved to be an impediment to them in the long run. The infamous reserve clause, which forced them to stay with one team, remained intact and would persist this way for approximately the next 85 years.

The Players League lasted just one season in 1890, and the Boston franchise won the championship. Games were well-attended in some cities, but generally, the league lacked the funding to continue, and its owners' lacked confidence in the project to continue beyond that one season. In 1891, the Boston and Philadelphia franchises joined the American Association after the Players' League failed, and both folded together with the American Association after the 1891 season. The Players League franchises in Brooklyn, New York, Chicago, and Pittsburgh merged with their National League counterparts after the 1890 season. It then reduced the number of major league teams and players, giving the remaining owners much greater leverage against the surviving player's attack. From a management angle, one benefit of the league was the construction of new ballparks. Several were used for a while by established major league clubs. The most prominent was the new Polo Grounds field, originally constructed as the Brotherhood Park for the New York Giants team of the Players League. It later became the home of the National League's New York Giants. They used the park from 1891 to 1957 (it was rebuilt in steel and concrete in 1911). It was also used as the home field for the New York Mets for their first two seasons while Shea Stadium was being built. It likewise was the site of many other famous sporting events throughout its 75 years of existence.

In Brooklyn, the Bridegrooms were merged with the one-year "Ward's Wonders." It is not anything the "Bridegrooms" ownership wanted, but only being in the National League for one year, they did not have much leverage yet. It would wind up costing them a lot of money.

Ward replaced William (Gunner) Mc Gunnigle, who had just won two championships. I would like to have been a fly on the wall when McGunnigle was told he was let go after winning two consecutive titles in two different leagues. Baseball is not a sport with sentiment. However, even though players' salaries were controlled to a level that caused the revolt, to begin with, the "Bridegrooms" owners paid players fairly and were not the root cause of the problem. That problem came from other cities and owners. The pennant race of 1890 was overshadowed by the clash between the National League and the Players League (or the Brotherhood League).

The National League formed a warfare committee headed by Chicago's Albert G. Spalding, who vowed to obliterate the rebellious league. They scheduled National League home games to compete with the home games of the Players League unswervingly. However, it was a two-edged sword (especially for teams like the "Bridegrooms"), as they had to compete in Brooklyn with the Players team and a new American Association club. The Blitzkrieg ploy worked, resulting in the Players League's demise after just one season. Charles Byrne was kind to his players. He was a team-oriented man who buoyed and helped head the battle with Albert G. Spalding to counter the upstart league. "There is no dodging the statement that Mr. Spalding and Mr. Byrne accomplished the downfall of the Players League," according to *Sporting Life*. But many baseball raconteurs felt that if Byrne had been in the National League sooner, he might have tempered some of the league's high-handed treatment of players that helped lead to the revolt. Brooklyn manager Bill McGunnigle in *Sporting Life* said that "If such a man ran the National League as the man, he worked for on the Brooklyn team, there would be no Brotherhood, there would be no cause for one, and it would be impossible to form one."

A curious side note was a challenge series between the "Bridegrooms" and the American Association champion from Louisville at the end of the regular season in 1890. The series was stopped after three wins each due to bad weather and a lack of interest!

John Montgomery Ward's Hall of Fame Plaque

CHAPTER TEN
Sojourn at Eastern Park

Charles Byrne, President of the Brooklyn "Bridegrooms", also known as just the "Grooms," was presented with an option to purchase a piece of land in East New York in late 1887. The property was bounded by Eastern Parkway (now Pitkin Avenue), Vesta Avenue (now Van Sinderen), Powell Street, and Sutter Avenue. However, he declined the chance because the city could extend Junius Street and Belmont Avenue through the plot. He was prophetic in his beliefs, as will be seen.

Street Map of Eastern Park After baseball left, streets were driven through Junius Street and Belmont Avenue just as Charles H. Byrne had predicted.

When the newly formed Brotherhood team (Ward's Wonders) needed a park for the 1890 season, John Montgomery

Ward jumped at the chance to lease the same piece of land from the Ridgewood Land and Improvement Company. This was a syndicate of businessmen headed by George W. Chauncey. As construction began, the Brooklyn Eagle claimed that "Brooklyn is to have the finest base ball grounds in the country." The new stadium was initially dubbed Atlantic Park in honor of a former champion Brooklyn team. Still, concerning the many bar owners who had already taken similar names for their watering hole establishments, the more common name of Eastern Park was chosen as the park was in the Brownsville section of East New York.

The Brooklyn Brotherhood squad provided good theater throughout 1890, finishing second place in the Players League behind Boston. But after that one season, the Players League disbanded, and "Ward's Wonders" were folded into and joined with Byrne's National League club.

According to the February 7. 1891 issue of the *Brooklyn Citizen*, on page 1, an agreement was reached to merge the two clubs "by forming a new company. It was to be done by the stockholders of the two old clubs individually. The new club is to be capitalized at $250,000, of which the stockholders of Brooklyn's limited will take $124,000, and the balance of $126,000 will go to Messrs. Byrne. Doyle and Abel. The new club will have a board of five directors, three of whom will be the National League trio. The property of each of the old organizations will be controlled by itself, and the only things to be turned over to the new club will be the contracts of players and the National League franchise. In return for these concessions, the new club will pay Messrs. Byrne, Doyle, and Abell $30,000 in cash and $10,000 out of the first year's receipts. The two old clubs will gradually wind up their business and eventually go out of existence. Eastern Park will be the home of Brooklyn's representative baseball club in the future. It was settled early this week by Presidents Goodwin and Chauncey, who acted respectively for the ball club and the Ridgewood Land and Improvement Company. A rental of about $7,000 per year was agreed upon on a lease to run five years. The Ridgewood Land and Improvement Company has acquired all the stands and other improvements at Eastern Park from Brooklyn's (limited), and the rental is reasonable. When President Goodwin rapped for order this morning, the following directors were present: Wendell Goodwin, John Wallace, Henry J. Robinson, end George J. Wirth. Attorney G. W. Murray of the firm of Anderson and Howland was on hand to guide matters legally. Mr. Goodwin detailed minutely everything he had done in the matter since he and President Byrne had agreed-upon terms. The financial arrangements had been made, and everything was in readiness for the plan to be adopted by the stockholders if the directors would so recommend. The directors formally adopted the plan and recommended it to the stockholders, who held their meeting immediately after the directors had finished. The stockholders confirmed the director's action, and both meetings were adjourned until Saturday of next week to complete details. Mr. Goodwin is now ready to talk with Mr. Byrne and arrange for the formation and incorporation of the new company."

The club inherited the land lease on Eastern Park. It remained there through the end of the 1897 season, completing their agreed-upon lease despite Charles Byrne's declaration during merger negotiations that he "did not purpose to desert so good and popular a ground as Washington Park for the furtherance of other people's real estate schemes." According to the *Brooklyn Eagle*. In 1890, baseball was not comparable to what we see today. There were no multiple streams of revenue as of today. There were no naming fees for fields, and television and radio did not exist along with their revenue flow. Endorsements and sponsorships also did not exist. The only form of profit was ticket sales at an average of 25 cents and a high of 50 cents. Sometimes in this era, we began to see billboards in the outfield for additional income. Parks also made income from renting their grounds for soccer, wild west shows, ice skating, and whatever else the public wanted, including amateur baseball. The wise magnate realized that the cranks' willingness to pay for a ticket was essential. Also, the quality and success of a team increased ticket sales. It was not a business for the slightly financially secure. (Though compared to other big businesses of the "Gilded Age" robber baron class, they were small change.) A good start in the spring was necessary for a team to succeed, and many players could not be afforded by their owners, so Abell and Byrne were first in line at the fire sale, so to speak. Of course, other acquisitions were made by trade, some successful, some not.

In Brooklyn, after championship seasons in 1889 in the American Association and again in the National League in 1890, winning appeared effortless and easy to replicate. They were not only a success on the field but also at the box office as well.

New to the equation was competition from Ward's Wonders at Eastern Park. Fan loyalty and ticket sale competition hurt the Bridegroom ownership team. Unfortunately, the players league attracted proprietors unsuited to own a baseball enterprise. Such owners had the potential to snuff out major league baseball at any given location. The three lead owners of the "Wonders" who now merged with the Bridegrooms were Wendall Goodwin,

Edwin Linton, and George Chauncey. None of these three had any business being in baseball. Chauncey had some baseball background, having played for the Excelsior club in the 1860s. He earned his living in real estate and had a vested interest in anything that increased the value of his property in Brooklyn. Baseball was not a priority, only a sideline.

George W. Chauncey.

ELECTION NOTICE.

A GENERAL MEETING OF THE stockholders of the BROOKLYN BALL CLUB will be held at the office of the counsel of the company, Messrs. KEODING & KIDDLE, 38 Park row, in the City of New York, on FRIDAY, January 29, 1892, at 3 o'clock in the afternoon of said day for the purpose of electing a board of directors for the ensuing year, the adoption of bylaws and the transaction of such other business as may lawfully come before the meeting.

Dated, Brooklyn, January 12, 1892.
WENDELL GOODWIN,
GEO. H. WIRTH,
F. A. ABELL,
JOSEPH J. DOYLE,
CHAS. H. BYRNE,
Corporators.

owners january 1892

Clipped By:

dodgerfan1 890
Sun, Jun 9, 2019

In 1890, Edward Linton supposedly owned half of East New York. His primary concern was developing East New York land, which was then in a remote location. As a Real Estate developer Linton had no problem promoting himself or his causes. He had a reputation of being contentious and challenging to deal with and usually offended someone daily. He was the proverbial bull in the China shop.

The third character in the triumvirate was Wendell Goodwin, an executive of the Kings County Elevated Railroad, which ran only one line but was the most lucrative in Brooklyn, carrying one and a half million passengers at a profit of $ $250,000 in 1890.

If you see no connection with baseball here, you are right, only real estate and railroad. Where did they build their field? Certainly not someplace convenient to the fans but in sparsely populated East New York to generate more railroad traffic and increase the value and sales of their real estate holdings there. They took no chances and built Eastern Park on land they already possessed and then leased the same plot under a company named the Ridgewood Land and Improvement Company, a syndicate headed by George W. Chauncey. This insured profit regardless of whether the team would succeed or not.

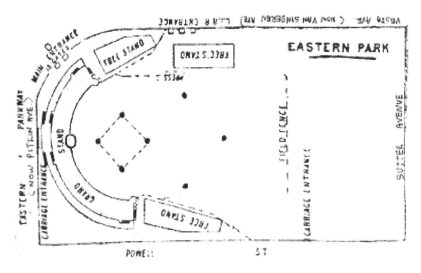

The layout of Eastern Park

Woodcut of Eastern Park

As the combined Brooklyn teams performed well below their expectations at the start of the 1891 season, so did Eastern Park, according to Charles Byrne. In mid-May, to improve the views of those in the upper deck and the back of the grandstand, Byrne made modifications to the park.

Byrne again oversaw substantial renovations at Eastern Park before the 1892 season. Most of the old grandstand from Washington Park was moved and rebuilt as a shaded pavilion opposite the first base. The bleachers near the third base were enlarged and elevated for a better view and rechristened "field seats" with a new price of 25 cents, half the old rate. Pavilion seats cost 50 cents, and grandstand seats 75 cents. The *Brooklyn Eagle* said the three-price system "worked to a charm." Not all the grandstand seats were lucrative, however. A system of patronage was in place where a great many politicians demanded complimentary annual passes, and, as Henry Chadwick wrote in the *Brooklyn Eagle*, "the majority of the political passes in question got into the hands of too rough an element to please the class of grandstand patrons who support the club by their money."

Despite these investments, the magnates were never happy with the move to Eastern Park in East New York. Gus Abell mainly had a jaded eye on finances and low attendance and looked forward to a move back to South Brooklyn. Rumors constantly circulated of a return to Washington Park from 1894 on.

Given the Eastern Park magnates' agenda, their foremost priority was for a consolidated club to play its games at Eastern Park so they could collect their land lease fees. They wanted it so badly that they promised to throw in $30,000 to sweeten up the pot plus $10,000 in first-year profits. Only $22,000 of the $30,000 was ever paid back. Abell did find a way to equalize the situation, though, as he took back shares from the new co-owners in lieu of the monies he laid out in their name. Their ownership percentage in the club shrunk, making it easier for them to be bought out later. Amazingly, Charles H. Byrne did not smell a rat here as he made very few bad choices as President of the Brooklyn team, but in the end, he agreed to take the money and abandon the much more desirable land in South Brooklyn.

Only known picture of Eastern Park

As reported in the *Brooklyn Eagle* of February 8, 1894, on page 8, we read that "According to President Byrne, it is quite true that Mr. Abell is going to take a stand that may make a deal of complicated trouble for the Brooklyn Base Ball club this season and Mr. Byrne thinks Mr. Abell is about right in the matter. Abell says he will withdraw unless other stockholders come forward and put up some of the cash required to run the club. Abell was tired of furnishing all the money when others profited largely from the enterprise. The corporation of the club is one with non-assessable stock, and there is no way for Abell to compel his partners to advance cash, but he may sell his stock, give it away, or apply for a receiver to be appointed to wind up the club's affairs. The prospects for money-making by the club this season are excellent, and as the other stockholders stand to win, they may come forward. Abell has threatened to stop furnishing all the money and get out, but his lawyer says he is in earnest this time. He does not want to be obliged to give up his interest, but it is purely a matter of business with him, and he will do so unless others share the burdens with him." He did not leave but claims that he lost $100,000 while connected with the Dodger team; though never stated, I think it is safe to say that the majority was lost during the merger with Eastern Park magnates from the players league.

1895 Mayo cut plug cards team set, Players, at Eastern Park are from authors Dodger Museum collection

The five-year lease on Eastern Park ended, and Gus Abell indicated that it would not be renewed. Abell and Byrne had long wanted to secure a more strategic location for a new field. There were supposedly five good sites suggested as desirable locations. Certainly, a new home would be secured after the following season ended.

Towards the end of the century, we saw hints that the National League forced the owners to consolidate as a form of peace with the Players League. They evidenced a willingness to put National League interests above their own. It all happened in their first year in the National League, so they probably did not want to make waves. It was a costly decision.

CHARLES H. EBBETS.

Charles H. Ebbets

The Brooklyn Team got rid of its contentious non-baseball-oriented owners when in 1897, George Chauncey acting as a trustee for the minority shareholders, sold their entire interests to Charles H. Ebbets. When Charles H. Byrne died shortly after that, Ebbets supposedly acquired his shares and became the majority owner of the team, or so he claimed (more on that will be discussed in a later chapter). Perhaps Chauncey's significant contribution to Dodger History was his recognizing Charles H. Ebbet's ability and passion for baseball and Brooklyn in 1897 when he sold out to him. Nobody worked harder than Charles H. Ebbets, and everyone knew it!

 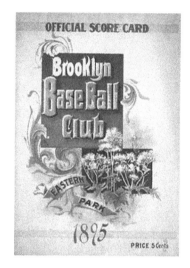

Official Programs from Eastern Park

Depressing Views of Former "Eastern Park" as seen today

CHAPTER ELEVEN

Joseph J. Doyle leaves

With the advent of the merger between the Brotherhood team with the "Bridegrooms," Joseph J. Doyle (one of the original owners) left the fold. Abell's "Central Club" gambling joint at 818 Broadway and Doyle's at 12 Ann Street were closed, heralding the beginning of the end of such "Society Clubs" in south Manhattan. Gambling dens were moving further north near Times Square, where the population and businesses were going. 818 Broadway was closed in 1890, and 12 Ann Street had the same fate around the same time.

Following the 1891 season, Joseph J. Doyle left the Brooklyn baseball organization after nine years as one of its directors and founders. There was some supposed argumentation between Doyle and Abell regarding the merger with the Players League group. The press, as usual, had various versions of what was happening or none.

In any event, Doyle sold two-thirds of his stock to Marks and Jolly, two gamblers from the Gloucester Racetrack in Massachusetts. The stock sale to Marks and Jolly was offered to Abell. He refused to endorse the sale or make the transfer because too many "sporting men" (aka gamblers) were already associated with the club. It is notable since both Abell and Doyle were "sporting men." Wendell Goodwin, who became an owner of the organization with the merging of Brooklyn Players League and National League clubs, offered to split the buying of the stock down the middle with Abell. He also offered to let him buy it outright. The problem here was the fear that Doyle and Byrne would leave to form a new team in the American Association. In hindsight, this would not have worked because the American Association closed its shop the next year and went out of business. Doyle offered an option to sell his stock, which ultimately led to his departure. At the Indianapolis meeting of the National League, it was determined what the Brooklyn stock was probably worth, which was more than Doyle's proposed option price. The underestimate forced Doyle into a corner. Perhaps due to the Marks and Jolly connection, he did not withdraw his option. He was stuck. Wendell Goodwin new owner from the merge, called his bluff and told him that if he were an honorable man, he would honor the option. If he didn't, he now had Goodwin as a business enemy.

From this point on, Doyle would have been squeezed by both Abell and Goodwin. Doyle had to sell as per his option. Doyle agreed to have a meeting with Abell to discuss the situation. Marks and Jolly came along with him. Doyle tried to get more out of Abell, but he told Doyle to honor his option.

A few months prior, the National League forced Abell to merge with the former Players League magnates from East New York after their first year in the league. Abell feared letting Goodwin gain more shares as he felt the owners connected with the East New York Real Estate conglomerate were unpredictable and unreliable.

After Abell made a deal with Doyle, Marks, and Jolly, he now owned 80 of the original 100 stocks and 41 of the 100 stocks with combined new owners from East New York. Doyle was given the option of buying out Abell but did not have the money or interest to do so, or probably both.

To complete the coup Abell next top aimed at Byrne since he was Doyle's brother-in-law and was now perceived to be an enemy. Byrne owned 20 of the old companies' stocks or 10 of the consolidated stocks. Abell (just as he would later do with the East New York group) demanded payment from Byrne for the monies he laid out for him. He took back these unpaid funds in the form of a stock re-purchase. Abell already owned the stocks by hypothecation. Byrne was left as president of the club in name only. Abell now had control of 51 of the 100 consolidated stocks and would get at least 13% more back as the East New York group did not pay monies laid out for them during the 5-year lease period at Eastern Park.

The new alignment announced in the papers had Byrne as president (with no control). Goodwin was vice-president and Abell secretary and treasurer. The board of directors included Abell, Byrne, Goodwin, Redding, and Kiddell. The last two were Abell's lawyers. All of Byrne's powers were now limited. It was further stipulated that Abell would have all National League voting powers and confer only with Goodwin. Byrne was left as a weak second delegate.

For the last six years of his life, Byrne was Abell's' puppet. Abell knew he needed a "wizard of oz" figure to hide behind. This faux image was created for public consumption only. The team's supporters liked the crisp cleanness of Byrne and his oratorical prowess. No longer could Byrne go to National League meetings without notifying Abell. Byrne claimed that he was relieved by the weight of the responsibilities being removed from his shoulders. Those around him knew better. He had to say that to save face.

Abell desperately needed this figurehead from 1883 to 1890 while still connected to gambling in New York City. Once his "Central Club" gambling joint at 818 Broadway was closed, Abell felt his oats. He no longer felt retribution from the law as a gambler since he was no longer involved in it. All rumors could successfully be denied.

He admitted a connection with a "society club" at Narragansett Pier, which was a false lead. That Society Club was operated by a bookie named Davy Johnson. Nobody apparently checked! Abell only admitted to having a farm in Newport, Rhode Island. The irony was he farmed gamblers not vegetables at his "Nautilus Club" in Newport.

On February 1, 1895, 10 and 12 Ann Street were sold to a bank. Doyle probably was gone by early 1892, as he had no more baseball or gambling interests in New York City or Brooklyn.

Doyle was last seen helping hammer out the details of the sale of Byrne's remaining shares in the club after Byrne died in 1898. From the reading of Byrne's final will, all that he owned were shares in the team not taken back by Abell. Byrne also claimed that the club still owed his brother and sister $2000 each for services rendered. Abell needed closure to finish a deal with Baltimore Orioles owners Harry von Der Horst and Ned Hanlon. Without the Byrne transaction, the Orioles would not be able to complete an arrangement to combine with the Brooklyn team. The Orioles had bad attendance in Baltimore, and the Brooklyn team was terrible. Merging was the perfect solution for both sides' problems.

Byrne had an apartment at 107 West Eleventh Street in New York City, which he rented, and had no other worldly possessions.

It proved that he never had any money, only the recognition given by the public. It is all Abell probably ever wanted from the start. Byrne played his role right to the end without anyone knowing the truth. Abell's organization was a windmill of misinformation and disinformation, as shown. It was all about form, not substance. The wizard was dead.

The last we ever hear of Cornelia Byrne Doyle was at the reading of Charles Byrne's will in 1898. The obituaries listed Byrne's sister Cornelia as being in White Plains, New York, which was the only clue that led to what happened to Doyle after his ownership of the team. Her other brother William G. Byrne was also present as the administrator of Byrnes's will.

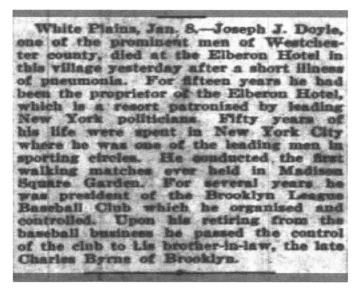

Above is the only available information about what happened to Doyle.

Research was done regarding Joseph J. Doyle in White Plains, New York. Still, as usual, only some type of legal action, census data, directory listing, or death notice would provide an answer. It appears Joe Doyle bought the Elberon Hotel in White Plains in 1891 and lived there until his death on January 8, 1906, from pneumonia. It was said that many leading politicians from New York City visited his establishment. As usual, none of these people were ever exacting or transparent. One incorrect fact in the above entry taken from the *Buffalo Commercial* on January 8, 1906, on page 1, was that Joseph J. Doyle was the baseball club president. That was Charles H. Byrne's role from the start to his death. From the directories of the time, we see Doyle's son Nicholas is listed as a clerk at the Elberon Hotel.

Given that, it seems apparent that this was only a hotel with nothing to do with gambling. Of course, this is only a supposition; perhaps gambling was also part of the offerings here. The only thing to suggest otherwise is having a son as a clerk. That would never have been needed in any of the other gambling joints of the time. Joseph J. Doyle probably had made enough money in gambling to retire to a less nerve-wracking business in his last 15 years. Doyle never had the wealth that Abell had. The only other information that could be gleaned was that the Elberon Hotel was on Court Street in White Plains and that by 1908 it had become a boarding house that provided furnished rooms. It was renamed "the Leonard" after its new owner W. H. Leonard. It was completely torn down in 1926. The White Plains Library and Historical Association were contacted and could offer no information besides a picture of the Elberon Hotel on Court Street and the Leonard information. They had no other details on any of the other Doyle family members.

Joseph J. Doyle's Elberon Hotel (the building in the middle of the picture) from 1891 to 1905 was in White Plains, New York, on Court Street.

CHAPTER TWELVE
"The Trolley Dodgers"

The only tangible item of historical significance that occurred while the team was at Eastern Park (1892-1897) was the nickname "Trolley Dodgers," used for the first time. During its tenure at Eastern Park, the team was barely above 500 (481-463). The team saw lower attendance than at Washington Park 1 (1883 to 1891), primarily due to a smaller population density than South Brooklyn and an inconvenient trip to get there. The team lost money and games over this period. Nothing great was going on in the field either.

It was reported for years that the "Trolley Dodger" moniker was an artifact from the 1880s. Historically this does not seem correct for several reasons. Before 1890 trolleys in Brooklyn were pulled by horses that moved at approximately 4 miles per hour.

They were not that hard to "Dodge". If you were to research newspapers at the time, there would be no "hue and cry" regarding horse-driven trolleys, causing an uproar of complaints from the citizenry of Brooklyn. The occasional incident caused some discourse, but this was more chance than prevalence. It wasn't until April 20, 1890, in the *Brooklyn Eagle*, on page 20, that we read that the first Electric Car line was started in

Brooklyn. It was officially known as "The Coney Island and Brooklyn Electric Line".

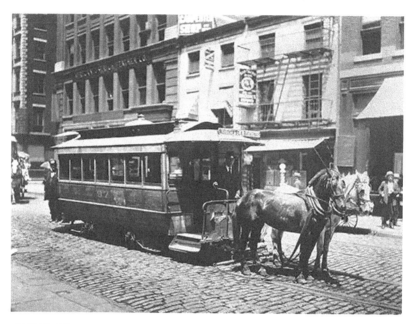

1890's Horse Powered Brooklyn Trolley meandered along at 4 miles per hour

It ran from the boulevard entrance to Prospect Park opposite the Parade ground to West Brighton, passing the Brighton Beach Hotel and race course approximately five miles long in the distance. There was only one car used initially, as seen below. These cars moved rapidly. It was estimated that they could go 15 to 20 miles an hour, far beyond the 4-mile-an-hour speeds the horses could do. Building up a fleet of Trolleys to "Dodge" would take more time.

An amusing story from the Brooklyn Eagle (not for him, though) was that Charles H. Byrne, President of the Brooklyn team, was himself hit by a trolley, according to the Brooklyn Eagle of July 12, 1896, on page 7. Though he unsuccessfully dodged the Trolley, it probably made him the original "Trolley Dodger" for the Brooklyn team! It was said he broke a rib in the melee with the Trolley. Due to this fracas, he spent the summer with Brooklyn team co-owner Gus Abell at his gambling casino, "The Nautilus Club" in Newport, Rhode Island.

First Electric Trolley in Brooklyn

It was said he broke a rib in the melee with the Trolley. Due to He also visited his sister Cornelia and brother-in-law Joseph J. Doyle (a former co-owner of the Brooklyn team from 1883 to 1892), who owned the "Elberon" hotel in White Plains, New York. Running the club during Byrne's absence was Charles H. Ebbets, future owner and builder of Ebbets Field, in 1913. He already had 13 years of being Byrne's assistant to guide him in 1896, starting with the club in May of 1883.

The actual origins of the "Trolley Dodgers" name can be found in the Philadelphia Press in response to the Brooklyn Press. There were quite a few rainouts in the early spring of 1895 while Brooklyn played Philadelphia in Philadelphia. The Brooklyn Press, ever searching for a storyline using a plethora of adjectives and adverbs as they pursued their trade, referred to the Philadelphia team as the "Rainmakers." Of course, the Philadelphia Press took umbrage and decided to strike back with their wordsmithing and fired back by calling the Brooklyn nothing but a bunch of "Trolley Dodgers." Obviously, this is at the level of third-graders razzing, but it stuck. Slow press days cause such mindless banter, apparently, but, in this case, it morphed into something else. Today we still have the Dodgers, but nowhere do we see "Rainmakers," fortunately. They didn't always dodge the rain in Philadelphia. In Brooklyn, they always dodged trolleys back then. *"The World"* (New York) May 1, 1895, claims the original quote happened a few weeks earlier. So, given this, April 1895 seems to be the origin of the Trolley Dodgers name.

> * * The "Rainmakers" and the "Trolley Dodgers" are the latest terms used by base ball writers to designate the Phillies and Brooklyns respectively.

Quote from Philadelphia Times May 4, 1895

> Brooklyn players are now known as trolley dodgers, and probably Dave Foutz is looked upon as the trolley pole, remarks an exchange.

Quote from Brooklyn Times April 26, 1895

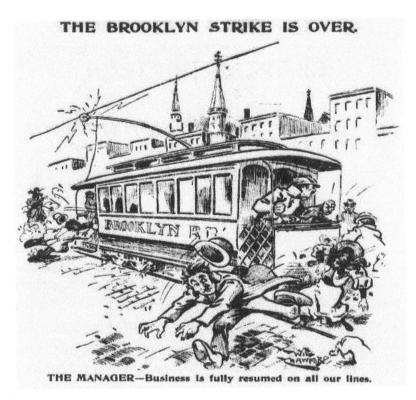

Typical Day in Brooklyn Trolley Heaven

CHAPTER THIRTEEN

Return to Washington Park

Well, this is perhaps a misnomer. As we left Washington Park 1, it was buried under 16 feet of dirt. The new site was diagonally across the street from the original Washington Park and is today the location of a Con Edison Facility. Now that Charles H. Ebbets was free of the self-serving real estate people from East New York, it was time to get out of Eastern Park. Like Charles Byrne had predicted, they continued two roads, Junius Street and Belmont Avenue, right through the heart of the field, creating four separate lots. In February 1897, the *Evening Telegram* reported that "The owners of the Brooklyn Baseball Club made a prospecting tour through the City of Churches yesterday, looking for a site for new grounds. They visited the place of the Brooklyn club's former greatness - Washington Park - and were impressed by the pensive manner in which the turf seemed to chide them forever leaving such a favorable location. The site back of the old grounds was visited, also Ambrose Park, some plots on the Nassau Railroad line, and other sections of real estate that may be graced this summer by the plaintive moan of the kicking ball player and the derisive howl of the lordly umpire. It is barely possible that not sufficient inducements can be made to cause the management to leave the present location at Eastern Park. However, it is maintained that it will not take much to get the team away from the rasping sawmills of Jamaica Bay." After team president Charles Byrne died early in 1898, Charles Ebbets took over as the Brooklyn Base Ball Club president. On the top of his to-do list was moving the team back from Eastern Park (where attendance had never been good) to South Brooklyn. After being offered several sites, Ebbets accepted a ten-year lease on a piece of land owned by the Litchfield estate. Its borders were First and Third Streets and Third and Fourth Avenues. The Brooklyn fans (except for a few fans from East New York) were delighted. The new park was diagonally across an intersection from the old Washington Park, where the team had won three pennants already. It would retain the same name. Historically it is known as Washington Park II.

SCENE AT THE OPENING OF THE WASHINGTON PARK GROUNDS.

Woodcut from the Brooklyn Eagle

Building costs for the new park of $20,000 were shared with the Nassau Electric and Brooklyn Heights L Railroad companies, which ran lines nearby and stood to gain a great deal of money from customers attending the games. Al Johnson, former president of the players league, was president of the rail lines and bought, graded, and built the park. It was agreed that the team would pay a $5000 a year land rent. ($2500 less than Eastern Park land rent) The rail lines would gain tremendous game ridership increases, so they decided to do the deal. Ebbets ensured that his main entrance was equidistant from both lines so as not to offend. Knowing how volatile the press could be, he provided a press box directly behind home plate. The club paid $80,000 in expenses to move the team, but Ebbets said he felt "thoroughly satisfied with the prospect in view" (according to the *Brooklyn Eagle*). Ebbets claims to have drafted the plans for the park himself which is probably an exaggeration as seen before.

Having already overseen the reconstruction of the grandstand a decade earlier, he had experience in that regard. The Brooklyn Eagle claims that Ebbets had architects design and prepare the plans while the loan negotiations were going on. Ebbets might have provided some ideas and suggestions but did not draft the plans himself. The roofed grandstand was pleasingly gabled. He set aside two rooms over the main entrance for his luxuriously fitted headquarters and office. The grandstand was placed in such a manner as to provide maximum protection from the sun. It arcs across the sky for the higher-priced tickets. Site preparation was minimal as the land was flat, with only two areas needing addressing.

Ebbets claimed he would complete the entire park in 45 days, even if it required electric lighting at night. He even opened a small on-site office to supervise operations and keep things running smoothly. Groundbreaking transpired on March 23, 1898, with Ebbets' 16-year-old daughter Lydie Mae Ebbets digging up the first shovel full of dirt. Ebbets was not out of the woods yet. Some adjustments were made to one of the grandstands. This adjustment caused the loss of 2000 high-priced grandstand seats. The fickle finger of fate, always needing to be propitiated, reared its' ugly head with a carpenter's strike happening simultaneously. Fortunately, the team began the season on the road gaining additional time to complete the park in time for the opener on April 30, 1898. Since Ebbets helped National League President Nick Young prepare the season schedule, this was probably more planning than luck. This Washington Park featured a grandstand able to seat 5,000, with 7,000 cheaper seats and "unlimited" standing room in the outfield. There was also room for 60 carriages and horses. Later pictures show Model "T" Fords parked in the outfield. Some 15,000 fans attended the opening, wherein Lydie Mae Ebbets raised the American flag. One immediately noticed that Ebbets had competition for seats from a large building across the street in the right field area. It was something that needed addressing soon.

On April 30, 1898, Brooklyn lost their long-awaited home opener, 6-4, to Philadelphia. However, they won the remaining five games of the homestand, playing in packed houses. Brooklyn outfielder James Sheckard met the new park with home runs in its first three games. With the help of the close right-field fence, James Sheckard would lead the National League in home runs for 1903 with 9. Harry Lumley would repeat the feat in 1904 with 9, as would first baseman Tim Jordan in both 1906 and 1908, with 12 Home Runs each year. It was a dead ball era with clunky bats and a mushy ball.

Original Washington Park 2 Programs and a signed pass from Gus Abell

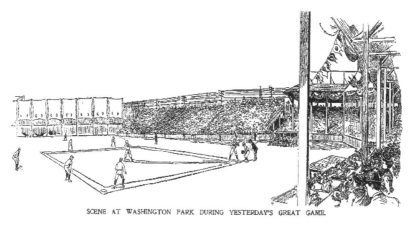

SCENE AT WASHINGTON PARK DURING YESTERDAY'S GREAT GAME

Opening Day 1899 (Note Canvas inserts in the right field known as "The Spite Wall" installed to prevent viewing of games as at Wrigley Field)

On Opening Day, 1899, we noticed canvas sheets installed (middle left) to prevent the intrusive fans on the roofs of the apartment buildings on First Street from viewing the game. The saloons and apartment dwellers across the street charged the fans a fee. High poles supporting canvas sheets known as the "Spite Wall" were added so as to prevent fans sitting in the "Ginney Flats" on First Street from watching the game. These existed through 1899, although the First Street fence was raised several feet. Just as at Wrigley Field, people sat on the fire escapes and the rooftops watching the game for free or at a reduced charge. The ground floor had saloons that sold them "growlers" of beer and hoisted the beer up on ropes to the cranks sitting above. This building was called the "Ginney Flats," pejoratively named after the Italians who lived there. Though not politically correct to call Italians "Ginneys" today, it was part of the jargon at that time.

The "Ginney Flats" viewing problem

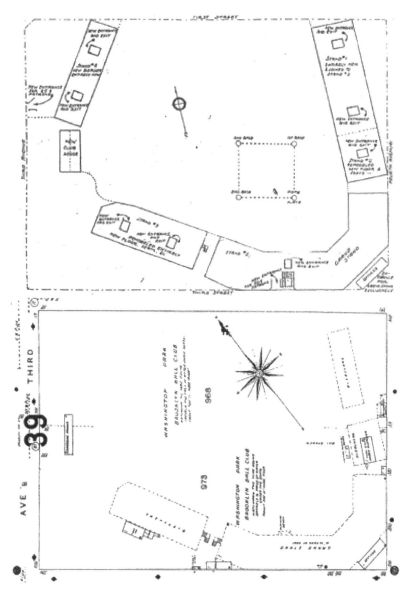

Original plans for the 1908 renovation are on the left.
Sanborn map from 1906 on the right,

Washington Park 2 (1898-1912)

The crowds continued to jam the stadium, seeing National League pennants brought back to Washington Park in 1899 and 1900. Even as the team became less competitive in years to come, attendance remained high.

Substantial renovations before the 1908 season, including thousands of new 25-cent bleacher seats along the Third Avenue side and upgrades of the existing bleachers to more expensive seats, saw capacity increase to 20,000. A well-appointed new clubhouse, including 24 lockers for home players and 20 for visitors, was also built behind the flagpole in left field. Innovative "dugouts" were provided for the shelter of players on the bench. When the "Brooklyns" left for a road trip on May 12, the transformation was already happening.

People waiting in line to buy tickets at Washington Park 2

During the trip, a new drainage system was installed to help prevent rain delays. Elevated seats improved views and the bleachers along the First Street side were shortened by 100 feet at each end. Those seats were moved to the Third Avenue side. Players had complained that fans were too close, and catchers did not like having fans in a direct line behind the pitcher and second base. Ebbets added every modification he could think of to enhance the fan experience.

Charles Ebbets was not considered a man of patience and was a "doer," not a "watcher" He was not pleased with manager Bill Barnie's results. He regularly criticized him with observations about his performance. Feeling he could do better, he appointed himself manager, amassing a 38-68 record that was far worse than Barnie's. That was the last time he ever managed! After thirty-five games, he let him go and replaced him with outfielder Mike Griffin who lasted four games with three losses.

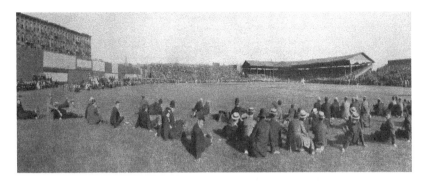

Sitting in the outfield at Washington Park 2 at the turn of the Century.

In 1909, in a scheme that would be echoed 100 years later at Shea Stadium and Yankee Stadium, the front of the grandstand was moved forward 15 feet, adding about 900 seats in "large and commodious" boxes for higher-paying customers, as well as an expanded press box. It reduced the distance between home plate and the grandstand to about 75 feet, still 25 feet more than most teams in the major leagues. This seating shift was also done at Dodger Stadium in recent times.

Despite all the enhancements and repairs over 15 seasons at Washington Park II, the wooden stands were tired by their last few years and started looking creaky, old-fashioned, obsolete, and inconsequential. In 1911 the idea of moving was floated by many writers. The *Brooklyn Eagle* even suggested replacing the old wooden park with a steel and concrete stadium. It was not until January 1912 that Charles H. Ebbets finally revealed his secretive plans to move to the other side of Prospect Park in an area called "Pigtown" to a new, majestic ballfield

Charles H. Ebbets

In December 1912, the New York Times and Brooklyn Eagle reported sadly on the dismantling of Washington Park II. The wooden grandstand and clubhouse were torn down, seemingly to make way for new streets and apartments. Recycling was the order of the day: "Most of the lumber has been sold to a Brooklyn firm, dealers in second-hand material, but the turnstiles are to be removed to Ebbets Field while the iron railings enclosing the boxes will be sent to Newark to be used in the park of the International League Club." However, a New Washington Park would come back to haunt them later in another baseball war. This time with the Federal League.

Washington Park 2 was carted away by horses in 1913, ending an era of wooden ballparks in Brooklyn.

CHAPTER FOURTEEN
Charles Byrne Passes Away

On January 4, 1898, Charles H. Byrne died from Bright's disease. Today is known as "Nephritis' (a type of kidney disease) at his home on 107 West Eleventh Street in New York City at 54. Team Doctor and personal physician Dr. H. C. McLean and various family members were also there to say goodbye to their beloved. Charles H. Byrne had been in a coma for about a week before he passed away.

In his 14 years in baseball (1883 to 1897), Byrne worked tirelessly in his efforts for the betterment of his cherished team and sport. Charles H. Byrne left behind a record that was unmatched among baseball executives of his day. Unfortunately, he never lived to see his team play at Washington Park 2 the following spring.

"From the year Mr. Byrne made his advent in the base ball arena, up to the year of his last illness, he was foremost in every movement that was calculated to benefit the national game," said Hall of Fame scribe Henry Chadwick of the *Brooklyn Eagle*.

Byrne always put the welfare of baseball above his own. "We are merely the backers of a sport that appeals to old and young," he said. "If we betray that trust, we betray the cardinal principle of the game that we control."

The Brooklyn baseball president's "apparent anxiety to conserve only the best interests of the national game was dear to him more than anything else on earth," *Sporting Life* said. "In that respect, he was easily the greatest magnate of them all."

Regarding the players league war, Sporting Life penned that "Like a born orator, he started in and electrified his hearers. There was no limit to his eloquence, and the good, solid English he hurled at the big gathering worked all to a pitch of enthusiasm that burst bounds when he told them in language unmistakable that he was in a position to say that Brooklyn had in all probability seen the last of the base ball war and that next season would mark a return to old principles and that Brooklynites would have only one club and one championship, and interest being undivided, another good spell of times would be quite a surety. This declaration was the windup of the night and was received with a general and united shout."

Byrne's club struggled in the 1890s, and he never won another pennant in his lifetime, but two were soon to follow his death in 1898. These National League championships happened in 1899 and 1900. Attendance, as expected, deteriorated at remote Eastern Park, where few people lived at the time. It was a bit of an inconvenience for the old fans to go there as well. The struggles took their toll on Byrne's health as well. The Brooklyn club president took a leave from his job and went to Hot Springs, Virginia, to try to heal his body. He couldn't, however, keep his mind off baseball. In the winter of 1897, despite ill health, he felt obligated to attend the National League meeting in Philadelphia.

THE MORNING HERALD, BALTIMORE, MONDAY APRIL 26, 1897.

MEN WHO CONTROL THE DESTINIES OF THE NATIONAL GAME.

Standing (left to right): E. E. Becker (Boston), Chris von der Ahe (St. Louis), Ned Hanlon (Baltimore), Frank Robison (Cleveland), Harry von der Horst (Baltimore), Joseph A. Hart (Chicago), J. Walter Spalding (Chicago), Harry Pulliam (Louisville), T. Hunt Stucky (Louisville), John Rogers (Philadelphia). *Seated:* John T. Brush (Cincinnati), Alfred J. Reach (Philadelphia), Gus Abell (Brooklyn), League president Nick Young, J. Earl Wagner (Washington), Stanley Robison (Cleveland), Charley Byrne (Brooklyn). (UMI)

Charles H. Byrne (bottom right) 8 months before he passed away. Gus Abell (bottom third from left)

Afterward, Byrne's health further worsened. He fell into a coma in late December 1897, right after Christmas. Byrne's funeral was held at St. Frances Xavier church on West Sixteenth Street on January 6, 1898 and was presided over by the Reverend Father Fink. Among those in attendance were well-known Sports figures, many of whom are in the Baseball Hall of Fame today. Players and magnates were both represented, several of the latter class being present from other cities. Most of those who attended the funeral had been personal friends and associates of Mr. Byrne during his baseball career, either in the old days of the American Association or later in the affairs of the National League.

The services at the church consisted of a simple mass for the dead, after which the casket was stationed in the vestibule to give the deceased's relatives and friends a chance to see the dead man's face for the last time. Flowers covered the coffin and took many more directly to Calvary Cemetery, where the interment occurred. The pallbearers, eight in number, were primarily well-known baseball men. They were Councilman Charles H. Ebbets, Nick Young, president of the National League; M. J. Griffin, captain of the Brooklyn team; Dr. H. C. McLean (team and personal physician); Patrick Powers, Al Reach of Philadelphia and Mr. Ferguson, who was claimed to be "one of Mr. Byrnes most intimate friends." Byrne was never married but was always claimed to be the most eligible bachelor in Brooklyn. Very few, except the pallbearers and the members of the family, left for the burial at Calvary Cemetery.

Some claim that few people came to his services but considering it was right after New Year's and winters are bitterly cold in New York City. We can assume that only those who felt closest to him showed up. Among other prominent characters in professional baseball present at the services were Gus Abell; Edward (Ned) Hanlon; president of the Baltimore Club; Henry Chadwick, a sportswriter from the Brooklyn Eagle newspaper; Walter Spalding; Harry M. Stevens; (America's foremost ballpark concessionaire); Ex-president John B, Day of the New York Club; Thomas Simpson assistant secretary of the Brooklyn Club team in the eighties and James Peebles (Cashier of the Brooklyn club in the 1880's.) Also in attendance were ex-umpire John Kelly and several ex-players who wanted to say goodbye to their friend and leader whom they appreciated. From all this, one can see that Charles H. Byrne was well cherished, respected, admired, and cared for by all he touched. (This is all according to the *Brooklyn Eagle* of January 6, 1898, on page 16)

Charles H. Byrne's name quickly faded from the history of baseball at the turn of the century but was founded on the sentiments of those involved in that sport in the late 1800s. No executive made more contributions to the early development of America's national game and the storied franchise known today as the Dodgers. Many feel he should be enshrined in the Baseball Hall of Fame in Cooperstown, New York.

As time waits for no one, a week later January 13, 1898, the Directors of the Brooklyn team met at the law offices of Alfred W. Kiddle located at the Potter building in New York City and elected Charles H. Ebbets as the president of the club to fill the unexpired term of former president Charles H. Byrne. Appropriately resolutions and salutations were drawn regarding their fallen friend and colleague Charles H. Byrne. (as per *New York Times* of January 13, 1898, page 4)

On March 2, 1898, Charles H. Byrne's last will and testament were filed in the Surrogate's office for probate. While rumored to be very wealthy, Byrne had no property, only 309 capital shares in the Brooklyn Base Ball Club. He left these in equal shares to his sister Cornelia M. Doyle of White Plains, New York, and his brother William G. Byrne of Brooklyn, who was also the executor of the will. They had an additional sister from various accounts, but she must have passed away prior as we find her name nowhere. He also left his brother and sister $2000 each for back salaries owed by the club. (as per the *Brooklyn Times* on March 2, 1898)

**The Terra Cotta "Potter Building" home of many of the
Brooklyn teams' legal landmarks**

A list of some of Charles H. Byrne's accolades would include:

1. Promoting a lady's day to encourage better behavior by the rowdy male contingency at games.
2. Introduced the concept of a rain check to provide insurance to the fans and to promote the club's ticket sales. Some confusion lies here while Byrne concocted the rain check. Ebbets later came up with a tear-off rain check attached to the ticket.
3. Established the first non-smoking section at a ballpark for Washington park fans.
4. Created the Coaches box that required coaches to be 75 feet from Home Plate.
5. Moved team first to the American Association, then the National League
6. Winning Championships first in the inter-state league in 1883, followed by a Championship in the American Association in 1889 and the National League in 1890.
7. Albert G. Spaulding helped beat back the Player's League challenge in 1890.
8. Scheduling the first tripleheader in major league history

Charles H. Byrne,
First President of the Brooklyn Baseball Club,
Who Died in 1897.

117

CHAPTER FIFTEEN

Syndicated Baseball

Syndicated Baseball was a practice in the National League in the 1890s. The exercise of this policy soon proved harmful. This happened when some of these magnates decided to favor one of their franchises at the expense of the other. The most infamous of these was what the brothers Frank and Stanley Robison did. They owned both the Cleveland Spiders and the St. Louis Perfectos and moved all the Spiders' best players to the St. Louis team before the 1899 season began. The Spiders wound up being the worst team in Major League Baseball history (20-134).

Other syndicate owners included John Brush, who had stakes in both the Cincinnati Reds and the New York Giants. The Brooklyn Bridegrooms and the Baltimore Orioles were also similarly connected. In all these cases, relations among owners led to players' movements highly damaging to one of the two cohort franchises. Thus, it became apparent that this practice had an inherent conflict of interest. Newspapers rightly lambasted the approach as the method shortchanged one set of fans. Syndicate ownership was outlawed and disappeared after the 1899 season when the National League shrunk by four teams.

Unbelievably the Brooklyn Bridegrooms were also connected with the Cleveland Spiders before the St. Louis deal happened. Harry Von der Horst, who later would transfer his players and interests to Brooklyn, said that the transfer of the entire Cleveland Spider club to Brooklyn openly confirmed "*The Sun's* story, published ten days ago, to the effect that a deal is talked of involving the transfer of the entire Cleveland team to Washington Park. Brooklyn, together with pooling of issues by Frank De Haas Robison and F. A. Abell. was correct in every detail. The scheme has been under consideration for some time past, and only a few days ago, Robison consulted me about It. He wanted to know whether I regarded the proposed deal as one that would result in profit, and I not only told him that it would but also urged him to make it. Some time ago, Mr. Abell offered to give me half of the controlling stock in the Brooklyn Club if I would put the Baltimore team at the old Eastern Park, but I couldn't see my way clear, as I had a pretty good thing where I was. If Abell makes that offer over again to Robison, I fully believe that something will come of It. The Cleveland Club is a loser in Forest City now and will never be able to make a success there again. The talk about locating the team in St. Louis and other places has had some truth in it, but the proposition to consolidate the Brooklyn and Cleveland teams, with headquarters at Washington Park, has got the league by the ears, and the club owners are discussing it from every standpoint. The fact is recognized that a winning team must be in Brooklyn next year, or that club will go by the board. It is an impossibility for Abell and Ebbets to build up a winner by securing minor league timber, for such a feat is not done by every manager and it takes years to accomplish it. Robison has a great team and a worthless franchise. Abell has a valuable plant and no team. These elements combined would develop a winner that would be of immense financial profit as Brooklyn patrons are hungry for good baseball". As fate would have it, no deal was consummated, leading to an even more fantastic deal with Baltimore.

Regarding an alleged syndicate to be executed between the Baltimore Orioles and the Brooklyn Bridegrooms, Baltimore players McGraw, Jennings, Kelley, and Keeler were said to have, formed a coalition to force the Brooklyn Club to pay them a bonus should the deal go through. According to the Baltimore American, McGraw, Jennings, and Kelley met in Baltimore and agreed that if a pennant-winning team in Brooklyn is to be such a Goldmine, they would like to have some share of the riches. At their meeting, the men agreed they would accept a suitable offer in salary and 10 percent of the net profits. "I think 10 percent is little enough," said McGraw. "If we are to be the stars that are to bring through the turnstiles the crowds of people, surely, we should share in some degree in money made through our own efforts. We want 10 percent and expect to stick by this demand." The presumption was that the players wanted the limit of salary prescribed by the league at $2,400. These players were known as the "Big Four" and similarly acted in unison with Von der Horst and Hanlon in Baltimore.

"President Von der Horst, who has been in Manhattan since the league meeting, was called to Baltimore yesterday by a telegram from Manager Hanlon. It is presumed that a conference will be held regarding the deal, which may or may not be closed. Ferdinand Abell has made a reputation for being the greatest purchaser of players connected with the national game. It was he who engineered the purchase of the Cleveland team years ago, just as he has been the promoter of the present deal, both of which were in their way the sensational events of baseball history. Mr. Abell also advanced most of the money whereby

Carruthers, Bushong, and the late Dave Foutz were transferred from St. Louis, a transaction which also created a sensation. Mr. Abell is still the principal owner of the club, although, as stated in yesterday's Eagle, he has delegated the financial management to President Ebbets. He is a man of the old school, pleasant alike to all, whether the other man is a league delegate or the porter in a hotel. In consequence, he is the easiest man to interview among the league owners and is, therefore exceedingly popular with newspapermen. Mr. Abell owns a house in Newport, where he spends most of his time during the summer. He delights in telling his friends of the large crops he raises each year on his farm, and during the league meeting at St. Louis last winter, when there was talk of war, jokingly exacted a promise from President Ebbets to secure for him two smooth bore cannons from the Navy Yard to he placed on his Newport property to frighten away the Spaniards." (from Brooklyn Eagle December 28, 1898)

As an aside, I would like to point out Abell's cover story about what he does in Newport in the summer on his supposed "farm." This further ties in with all the other unsubstantiated rumors and gossip. Abell was farming gamblers, not vegetables, in Newport, Rhode Island. No one got the inside joke at the time.

For almost three months, there appeared to be a snag blamed on Ebbets and the Byrne estate. Finally, on February 11, 1898, we have clarity, as seen from the *Sun* newspaper of that date "There will be no further haggling over the completion of details In the Brooklyn-Baltimore baseball consolidation. After a long conference at the law offices of Redding and Kiddle in the Potter building yesterday, a plan of action was decided on that clinches the deal beyond a doubt. Von der Horst and Hanlon, owners of the Baltimore Club, with their attorney Thomas R. Clendenen. were on hand early and ready as usual to close the matter. F. A.

Abell, C.H. Ebbets, W. G. Byrne, and Joseph Doyle, who jointly hold all of the Brooklyn Club's stock, came in about 2 o'clock. Abell and Ebbets were represented by Lawyer Kiddle while Byrne and Doyle had Lawyer Moss to advise them. In short, the conclave assumed such a legal aspect that it was likened to an investigation of some deeply laid mystery. Once and for all, Byrne and Doyle were requested to hand over 8 percent of the club's stock for $10,000. Byrne stated that he was unable to find sixty-one shares. Then the pressure was brought to bear on him to make an arrangement whereby he could bridge over this item and make the signing of papers possible. After two hours of further argument, Lawyer Redding made this announcement to the reporters: "All Interested parties have reached a final and amicable agreement. "As Byrne is still unable to find a certificate of sixty-one shares of the Brooklyn Club's stock, it has been decided that he must secure a proper order from the court of New Jersey to protect the Brooklyn Club against loss. This is necessary because the club is incorporated under the laws of the State of New Jersey. The method of procedure will be to ask the court to order to issue of a new certificate of stock to be substituted for the missing shares. The court must also assign a value to the stock and define the character of bond to be given by Byrne. This arrangement has been accepted by Byrne as entirety satisfactory and he will make an application to the court at once. It will take perhaps two or three days to get a decision, after which Byrne will turn over his holdings and receive $10,000 In cash. By this method, the last obstacle to the completion of the deal has been removed and the papers are as good as signed. Byrne will experience no trouble in getting a new certificate. We do this to protect ourselves legally". When this statement was made, all the baseball men united in saying that the deal was closed. Von der Horst and Abell both said they were satisfied. Abell remarked: "I am happy tonight. There has been no end of worry about this matter, and at times things looked squally. But It's all over now and the people of Brooklyn have secured a grand ball team. I have no statements to make further about the hurdles and blockades which were once so thickly strewn in my path, for everything has been settled satisfactorily. From now on, the cranks can pay attention to the doings of Manager Hanlon and his crack players. Von der Horst was all smiles and shook hands cordially with Byrne, Ebbets and the others". He said, "This whole deal and its details originated in *"The Sun"* and when the suggestion was made to Abell and myself at the League meetings in November. It was immediately taken up not only by the Brooklyn and Baltimore clubs but by the entire League. The placing of a strong team In Greater New York is due more to the efforts of that newspaper than to any of the magnates. Am I not right Abell? Those are the facts was Abell's reply. It was *"The Sun"* that brought us together in the first place. The deal was outlined from the start. In almost the same way that it has been completed. Baseball will leap once more into favor because of this move."

The following year saw the realization that a twelve-club circuit was cumbersome and impracticable from both a performance level and a financial point of view. With so many competitors and Brooklyn now with a powerful team, interest in the race was lost by the three or four clubs near the bottom of the second division. Their attendance fell as well. The only remedy in sight was a reduction in the league's size and plans to that end were laid in 1899. The assignment of the stars of the Baltimore team to Brooklyn was one of the first steps taken, and astute observers began to see the writing on the wall. A mighty upheaval came from cities that thought they were condemned. General opinion applied the ax to Baltimore, Washington, Cleveland, and Louisville, which proved accurate. At the end of 1900, they were no longer in the National League, and we were left with only eight teams in the National League for the next 62 years.

Of course, after all the fur flew and the dust settled, one might think this would be the end of this part of the story. Not So! The New York contingency in the National League was miffed by all this and wound-up losing money because the cranks would prefer to go to Washington Park and see a winner play. In that regard, we see in the New York Sun of January 9, 1900, the following quote "It has been stated by the League Magnates notably Brush, Soden, Wagner, and Freedman that the Brooklyn Club is not a desirable member of the League and if it were possible the Washington Club would be included in the proposed Eight Club Circuit instead. This assertion has been prompted by the enmity of the New York Club to the "Brooklyns," chiefly because the latter produced a championship team last season. The New York Club's president has openly admitted that he wants all the Greater New York territory to himself, but this appears to be an impossibility. As evidence that the enemies of the Brooklyn club have not been speaking by the card. F.A. Abell and C. H. Ebbets, who hold half of the Brooklyn club's capital stock, have wiped out a bond and mortgage amounting to $50,000, which leaves the books of the club in clean shape".

Harry Von der Horst

In 1895, when the Brooklyn club was in financial straits, there was a bond issue to tide things over. No assistance was asked from the National League, however, and the magnates were loud in the praises of the Brooklyn owners. When the Brooklyn-Baltimore consolidation was consummated last year, part of the agreement was that Abell and Ebbets should wipe out the debts of the old Brooklyn club while Von der Horst and

125

Hanlon should look after the obligations of the old Baltimore club. Having enjoyed a profitable season last year at Washington Park, the Brooklyn officials refused to tell when asked how much money was made. It was roughly estimated, however, that $45,000 was a fair figure. But it now turns out that nearly twice that amount was locked away in the safe. The bond issue has five years to run yet, but with money in hand, Abell and Ebbets thought it best to settle accounts without further delay.

It is understood that the cash is in the hands of the club's attorney and that after Directors Abell, Ebbets, Hanlon, and Von der Horst sanction the payment, legal papers will be turned over to the creditors, the chief one being Abell, who has voluntarily furnished money for Brooklyn's club for years. When the money has been formally paid, one debt of minor consequence will remain that cannot be settled before a given time. Though he has carefully refused to discuss the affairs of the Brooklyn Club since the Freedman crowd started to injure it and possibly drive it out of the league, Abell consented yesterday to make these remarks: "The Brooklyn Club since its organization eighteen years ago, has always stood upon its own bottom. In that time, the club has expended $100,000 for ball players. We have never asked the league to strengthen our team gratis and have always paid for everything we wanted. Since joining the National League in 1890, we have met all obligations and have always acceded to the demands of other clubs. Personally, I have stood a loss up to the beginning of last season amounting to nearly $80,000, yet I never asked the League to help me out, as the New York club did at one time, when with others, I subscribed my share to keep it alive.

To assist the league in its efforts to smooth matters over after the disastrous Brotherhood war in 1890, which the

Brooklyn club took no part in bringing it on. The late Mr. Byrne and I agreed to consolidate with the Brooklyn Brotherhood club. At old Washington Park we made plenty of money, but we sacrificed that good stand for the League's benefit. We gave up 49 percent of our stock to the Brotherhood club people and moved out to Eastern Park, which proved out to be a white elephant from the start. Attendance at Eastern Park varied from 180,000 to 230,000 annually. Losing money in bundles by this arrangement, we never asked the League for a dollar but plugged along as well as we could."

"Finding that we could not get out of the mire, we bought out the Brotherhood people and Mr. Ebbets and I proceeded to build our new grounds at Washington Park, which cost us close to $30,000. In accomplishing this object, we once again refrained from asking our partners in the League for financial aid preferring to go along the same old way. Then as a final effort to benefit the League at our own expense, we made the deal with the Baltimore club which incidentally involved the payment of $10,000 cash to the Byrne Estate and produced what the public had demanded all along-a pennant winner.

Last season the Brooklyn club paid the biggest salaries in the country. We spared no expense to give first class baseball, and we won the League pennant because we had the best ball team in the land. In return for this we made money, which I believe, was a reward for our persistence."

"As in the past, the Brooklyn club does not ask for any assistance from the League. We are ready to pay the best prices for the best players and willing to put up our share toward reducing the circuit and building up the game. All we desire is a fair deal from the men who have matters in charge. Our record speaks for itself. And the support we received last year was good enough proof that we enjoy the confidence of baseball patrons in this city. The gentlemen of the league may beat us in hotel corridors in the winter months, but we will return the compliment on the diamond next summer. The public wants winning baseball and is already disgusted with the methods of the men who control the game."

Abell's statement does not agree with the remarks of Freedman that the Brooklyn club should be disciplined for the good of baseball. While the Brooklyn club with a pennant winner was coining money the prior year, the New York club with a poor team rolled up a loss that "was the greatest in the history of the organization." Some might say the New York club was jealous and needed to find a demon to blame. Some were probably right.

Harry Von der Horst

CHAPTER SIXTEEN

Harry Von der Horst
and Ned Hanlon

Harry Von der Horst (1854-1905) was a Baltimore brewer who had owned the Orioles since they had been in the American Association with Byrne's and Abell's team. He was the owner of the Eagle brewery Company on Bel Air Road in Baltimore, Maryland. Apparently, a Golden Eagle was chosen as the company's symbol because "Horst" is a German word meaning "Eagle's Nest." Harry's father, John, came from Germany and brought all his old-world knowledge of beer making. Harry, however, had no mind for the business and was thoroughly ensnared by baseball instead. It was something an old brew master from Germany would never understand. He probably didn't know of or care about baseball, either.

VON DER HORST'S LAGER BEER BREWERY BELL AIR ROAD.

Harry Von der Horst wasn't very successful at baseball until he met up with Ned Hanlon, who was suggested to him as a managerial candidate. Hanlon was only 34 at the time. He was a member of John Montgomery Ward's team in the players league at Eastern Park. Following that stop, Hanlon had been player-manager of the Pittsburg (no "h" back then) Pirates. After trying to control a hard-drinking team without success, he had to throw in the towel and go back to just playing centerfield. An injury to a tendon sidelined him hence making him available. Von der Horst asked permission to talk to Hanlon, and Pittsburg was more than willing to dump the $5,000 salary of an aging veteran.

Edward Hugh Hanlon was described as quiet and just listened to conversations gathering whatever he needed from just that. He never spoke much, just evaluated. Not surprisingly, he was given the nickname "Foxy Ned" due to his demeanor. He was strong-minded, thorough, diligent, and seemingly unaffected by others' thoughts. He never struck back at his players. These were considered leadership qualities. Others seemed to want to please him. Von der Horst met with Hanlon and decided to give him a contract. Baltimore had never won anything before, so he was desperate for results.

Hanlon met with his new charges singly and in groups seeking a buy-in to his philosophies. He also was a strict adherent to "scientific" baseball. It was something very well understood today but not so much back then. He claimed to wake up at night thinking of plays and ploys to catch the opposition off guard. He then wrote it down in a book to apply at some future date. These innovations included a sacrifice bunt, hit and run play, and the suicide squeeze play. He also had the dirt in front of home plate tamped down to make it hard and trained his players to hit hard down on the ball for a base hit. It became known as the "Baltimore Chop." Many players considered these ploys unmanly, but they worked!

Whenever you see any of these plays executed today, remember to think of the name Ned Hanlon who institutionalized them for baseball. He trained the Baltimore team to be practitioners of these maneuvers. This, of course, led to winning, as nobody else understood it.

Von der Horst had some reservations about Hanlon for two reasons. The first was that Hanlon wanted total unquestioning control. It always grated Von der Horst the wrong way as he was a hands-on guy. Later, Hanlon gave Von der Horst $7000 for a 25% interest in the club. When they won (and win, they did with three straight championships in 1894, 1895, and 1896), Hanlon asked for 25% of the profits. Von der Horst considered the $7000 Hanlon gave him loan and paid it back rather than split the profits. These two items peeved both men and would come to bear later in Brooklyn.

Ned Hanlon 1857-1937

After these championships, Baltimore cranks stopped attending games. It was a competitive squad which would shortly mean their demise.

There was a natural attraction because each side had what the other team wanted. Nobody was surprised by Von der Horst's interest. No one could have imagined a more suitable arrangement. Harry put his brewery in a beer trust of twenty-one Baltimore breweries known as the Maryland Brewing Company.

Not having any connections left in Baltimore, Von der Horst moved to Brooklyn and joined in with the Abell and Ebbets. He also brought his best players and manager Ned Hanlon along with him to reprise his championship seasons in Baltimore.

At the time, a touring vaudevillian troupe with the moniker of "Hanlon's Superbas" appeared many times in Brooklyn. In their best juvenile manner, the newspaper pundits did not miss a heartbeat and began calling the baseball team "Hanlon's Superbas." Hanlon did what was expected and won the 1899 and 1900 National League Championships. Fans seemed wary about seeing Hanlon and Von der Horst and some of their players in Brooklyn, which may have negatively influenced attendance. Syndication was not understood or liked well by the fans, and the National League banned the practice the very next year. Hanlon stayed with Brooklyn until 1905, when he left to manage Cincinnati. He could not find the lightning in the bottle again, but with the birth of the American League and the raiding of Brooklyn players by the new league Hanlon was doomed. Byron Bancroft Johnson, president of the American League, declared open war on the National League for not recognizing them as a major league. Johnsons' representatives raided the ranks of the National League and stole many-valued stars. Jones. McGinnity and Cross were taken from the Brooklyn team. The loss of these critical players caused the Superbas to slip to third place in 1901. In 1902 additional raids took away Kelly, Sheckard, Keeler, Donovan, Daly, and McGuire. This open warfare had done more than take away valuable players. It robbed Abell and Von der Horst of their enthusiasm, and even though Brooklyn finished in second place in 1902, business fell off at the turnstiles. Abell sold out to Ebbets but was not paid in full until 1907. Ebbets was not a man of money, and no endless profits from gambling and beer lined his pockets with gold.

Then began the death struggle between Hanlon and Ebbets. Von der Horst, who had bad health, announced that he was pulling out of baseball and selling his stock in the Brooklyn team. Hanlon seemed to want to take the team back to Baltimore.

Ebbets still had faith in Brooklyn. Ebbets had no additional money after the agreement with the syndicate from East New York. Still, they somehow got the necessary funding to buy out Harry Von der Horst from Henry J. Medicus, a Brooklyn furniture dealer and a bowling league buddy. The deal, however, was held up by legal complications until it was settled in 1907. There was still hostility between Von der Horst and Hanlon. Because of that, Von der Horst was more inclined to sell to Ebbets, which eventually his estate did as the dispute went past his death.

Now in virtual control, Ebbets increased his salary from $7,500 to $10,000 while decreasing Hanlons' from $11,000 to $7,500. Why Hanlon didn't leave after this coup is unknown, he probably could have found reasonable offers in the American League (given his winning track record) and their team in Baltimore, which eventually moved and evolved into the New York Yankees. However, Hanlon left Brooklyn in 1905, the same year Harry Von der Horst died. As a manager, he won five championships and provided the seeds for analytical scientific baseball. His first three championships were in Baltimore and the last two in Brooklyn. As one might expect, he is enshrined in the National Baseball Hall of Fame in Cooperstown, New York.

CHAPTER SEVENTEEN
Charles Hercules Ebbets

Charles H. Ebbets was born October 29, 1859, to John B. Ebbets (1824-1888) and Ann Maria Quick Ebbets (1824-1871). He was born at home, which was 31 Clark Street in Manhattan. This area is known as SoHo, bounded by Broadway, Canal Street, and Houston Streets. Houston street was pronounced house-ton by the local denizens. They never heard of Sam Houston from Texas or didn't care. Ebbets came from an old Dutch family that arrived in New Amsterdam in the late 1600s. Charles' father, John, was involved in the liquor business in varying capacities. His grandfather was purportedly friends with Peter Stuyvesant. According to Ebbets wife Minnie, some years later, his granddad also owned a cow pasture that today is the site of Cooper Union.

In many historical documents, Ebbets' grand uncle Daniel has been mistaken for his father, John. Daniel was a prominent New York Banker who worked for either the Union Saving Bank or the Dime Savings Bank, depending on your source. Whichever bank, it was the one that Alexander J. Cartwright of baseball lore worked at as well. Both his cousins, once removed, Edward and Arthur, played for the Knickerbockers in the 1840s.

In some cases, it was claimed that Charles Ebbets played ball, but it was only his relatives that did so.

In 1871, the Ebbets family moved to Astoria, Queens, around the time of the death of his mother. Very little is known about the period from 1871 to his association with the Brooklyn Base Ball club in May 1883. There are discrepancies in that Ebbets created a myth rather than tell the truth as the legend was more interesting. Maybe we can be kind and blame it on a faulty memory (or both!). In reminisces, he claimed that he had several jobs before baseball. The first was at the architectural firm of William T. Beer at 896 Broadway, not too far from Gus Abell's "Central Club" gambling joint at 818 Broadway. His uncle William T. Beer was the proprietor there, so the job probably had a component of nepotism. Ebbets, ever the fibber, claimed to have drawn up the plans for the ritzy Metropolitan Hotel and Niblo's Garden, a famous theater at the time.

Given that these two venues finished their renovation in early 1870, Ebbets would have been in his early teens at the time. He probably was a clerk and sharpened pencils at best. If we peruse Directories of the time, we will find Charles Ebbets listed as a clerk or involved in wine sales. The wine sales wouldn't be surprising given his father's background, but this is something never admitted to by Ebbets himself.

After leaving his uncle's firm, he worked for Dick and Fitzgerald at 18 Ann Street, which was just three doors down from Joseph Doyle's "society club" (aka Gambling joint) at 12 Ann Street. Ann Street is very narrow and only three blocks long, so it wouldn't be surprising to meet Doyle, Byrne, and Abell in advance of the claim that his brother Jack recommended that he take the job with the nascent ball club. He was probably a clerk and made sales, including the door-to-door variety, given the many stories promulgated at the time. The last job Ebbets admitted to was working for Frank Leslie's publications as a subscription clerk at 537 Pearl Street in New York City. Frank Leslie was the pen name of Henry Carter (1821-1880), the son of a wealthy English glovemaker. Carter had taken up the craft of wood engraving over his father's wishes and migrated to New York City, arriving in 1848. Carter adopted the Frank Leslie moniker immediately upon his arrival and could not find a job as an illustrator with an established newspaper in the city. As a start, he was forced to open his own business, a small engraving shop on Broadway.

In January 18, 1913, issue of the *Brooklyn Eagle*, Ebbets described himself as an "assistant secretary and handyman," a jack of all trades. In an article from the New York Daily News on September 28, 1941, Ebbets' wife Minnie claimed she would "like to shoot the person who started the story that Charlie got his start with the club by selling programs and that I also eked out the family income by washing club uniforms. I was too busy with children to wash uniforms and too little to lift a wet one. But one day, the uniforms wouldn't dry at the park, and the boys brought them up to the house and hung them on my line," starting a story that wouldn't die. It was also rumored that Charles Ebbets printed the programs under the grandstands. He did anything Charles Byrne asked him to do as he loved what he did, no matter what it took to accomplish. People would see him wiping down seats, selling tickets, a clerk, usher, business manager, road boss, and other various and sundry jobs.

Unfortunately, sports scribes who were potentates of the word, had sluggish days with no stories. They had to figure out a way to assault pronouns and nouns with adjectives and

137

adverbs. As a result, all manners of stories appeared like the two above. Ebbets also told tales as a raconteur of the ersatz, so we are sometimes left with a shoulder shrug. Maybe Ebbets should have been a reporter as he seemed to understand some of their techniques and practiced them quite well. As a politician, he would understand how to simultaneously speak out of both sides of his mouth and pontificate, expound, expand, exaggerate and illustrate at a moment's notice! He was, however, a hard worker and dedicated to Brooklyn and its' ball club. No one could deny that.

Ebbets formal education went only as far as an eighth-grade public school. Ebbets primary education happened by observing Charles H. Byrne for many years as an apprentice. During these thirteen years, he asked questions about Byrne's decisions and the logic used to come to those conclusions. He learned every job at the park by doing them all. He met all the other magnates in the National League and learned their quirks.

Ebbets became a politician and won several races. He was a member of various fraternal and secret societies. Heavy involvement in bowling leagues and cycling in Brooklyn existed. All these skills and connections would later be used to temper and shore up his leadership as the owner of the Brooklyn team.

Both Byrne and Ebbets made league schedules for the National League, though to what extent each was involved is unclear, as once Byrne died in 1898, no one remained to question Ebbets assertions. The worst problem with setting up the schedules was considering train schedules, which changed.

Just as the United States started with 13 colonies, all strung along the Atlantic Ocean. The National League began with 12 (then 8) teams in the American Northeast. Expansion in both baseball and the United States followed the population shift to the growing cities in the west. Better forms of travel other than trains were yet to be invented. Interstate Highways with Greyhound Buses and airplanes did not exist in this world. Local travel was trolleys, elevated trains, or by foot or bicycle. For long-distance travel, locomotives were all that were available at the time. Their timetables were subject to change, so sometimes, teams did not get to their venues on time. Schedules were subject to the whim and vagaries of the various train companies.

Ebbets did not become an owner until late 1897, with stock bought from Chauncey and his East New York real estate cronies. It was a wonder that he could purchase back what was initially 49% of the estimated capitalization of $250,000, which would amount to $147,000 for only $25,000. Abell had taken back some stock from the East New York Group by hypothecation. By 1897 their percentage of ownership shrank from 49% to 37%, making their owned stock value at $92,500. There was also the matter of the $8000 of the original pledged money that was never paid back, which Abell took back by forfeiture of stock. (all these numbers are contentious as no one has seen ledger sheets. These seem to make the most sense) Probably the group didn't care any longer as they had already collected back their rental fees from the Eastern Park land and drew more people to the area to enhance their real estate values. From the start, this was their primary aim. They also still had the four lots that Eastern Park was composed of. They wasted no time running roads through Junius and Belmont Streets and created four separate lots for sale, something Charles H. Byrne had already predicted seven years earlier.

Wendell Goodwin of the East New York group was in poor health and had some alleged financial problems, so he was probably amenable to getting the team off his proverbial plate. With all his wit and guile, Abell could not wrench control from the East New York group, so it is surprising that Ebbets pulled it off. Even more surprising was where Ebbets found the money. To do so was impossible as Ebbets came from no money and had none to speak of. Many have tried to find the money but couldn't even account for half of it. It is purely speculation on my part, but maybe Abell knowing the fondness Chauncey held Ebbets in, was somehow in the mix. Abell needed to get rid of his erstwhile partners, so he surreptitiously provided the funds. Of course, they wouldn't admit it so as not to embarrass Chauncey, who was by all accounts a gentleman. Perhaps a cover story was needed, something both Abell and Ebbets weren't averse to doing. Just as Byrne was dying, Ebbets called a press conference at the Clarendon Hotel to announce that he was in total control. It was a bald-faced lie. Ebbets supposedly had an option to buy out the rest of Abell's stock by February 1, 1898, which was not taken. (His actual take-over did not happen until 1907) It was then stated that Abell was reticent to leave as he had so many friends among the magnates of the National League. We will never know the answer here, but it might have been a show set up to appease Chauncey, who everyone seemed to like.

"At one time, Mr. Abell threatened seriously to leave baseball entirely and let the club get along as best it could, but the lie was smoothed over, and he continued as the human war chest. He was a man who could be treated only in certain ways, and, unless you knew those ways, you never got what you wanted, but to those familiar with his peculiarities, he was not as hard to deal with as the public might have supposed." The above quote *from the Brooklyn Eagle* on March 1, 1913, gives insight into Abell and Ebbets relationship. Ebbets said it with a glimmer in his eye. We will never know how many times Ebbets tapped this war chest. Ebbets was poor and had no assets from beer, Gambling, finance, insurance, railroads, and oil. It is safe to say that he had to fend for himself early on. Abell's' money disappeared after 1903, and Ebbets started to be called "cheap" and "miserly." He was truly living on the edge, pasting things together daily. Abell had no family, and most of his siblings had died by this time. His wife, Almira, would pass in 1908. His only child was the Brooklyn team, as he was done with Gambling after the sale of his "Nautilus Club" in Newport, Rhode Island, to Richard Canfield just before the turn of the century.

President Charles H. Ebbets acquired the interests of the Von der Horst estate, Ned Hanlon, and Gus Abell in the old Baltimore Club of the National League and American Association and their interests in the present Brooklyn Club organization. In November of 1907, we read that Ebbets got control of the Brooklyn team and acquired Hanlon and Von der Horst's Baltimore interests. It was claimed that for the first time since the National League shrank to eight teams, the Brooklyn Club was owned entirely by residents of the City of Churches due to negotiations that had just been completed. Exactly how, was never explained. This transfer ended all the lawsuits started by the minority stockholders of the "Superbas" and left Charles H. Ebbets in control. Under the new arrangement, Ebbets controlled sixty percent of the stock, and his son Charles H., Jr., secretary of the club, had a ten percent interest. Treasurer Henry Medicus, a Brooklyn furniture store owner and a member of Charlie's bowling league from Brooklyn, controlled the other 30 percent of the stock. Ebbets paid Abell $20,000 with only $500 initially paid and the rest in notes. Hanlon was paid $10,000.

According to Ebbets, the present officers of the Brooklyn team were kept. It was claimed that "the fight for the ownership of the Brooklyn Club has been of long-standing and from its lawyers reaped large fees. For seven years, the matter had been in the courts, and the previous April, Ebbets was forbidden from selling any of the club's property and accepting any big offers for his stars. Hanlon's grievance was that Ebbets was copping all the profits and paying himself salaries as president and general manager. Abell, for a time, held aloof from the controversy but finally allied himself with his former manager Hanlon. From Abell, the proposition to make an amicable settlement of the dispute was received and thus put an end to all the litigation. The overtures were made the previous Friday, and once the bird of peace was near the warring magnates, it was quickly captured."

Abell was gone after 25 years and would only live six more years at his home in West Yarmouth, Massachusetts. It was time for Ebbets to finally make his mark on the History of the Dodgers.

CHAPTER EIGHTEEN

The War with the American League

With the demise of the Player's League after the 1890 season, the supremacy of the National League went unchallenged. They were arrogant in their manner because they thought they would go unchecked, keeping the maximum salary at the $2400 level. They ensured they left the reserve clause intact so players could not move to other teams. As if in a trance, they assumed this would go on forever. Something was simmering in the west, however (Midwest today). Things were about to change.

The senior circuit's shady conceit was matched only by its disarray. No one minded the store. They were neither fearful nor aware that an unknown league was about to charge forth and challenge their pre-eminence. After the death of the American Association in 1891 and the downsizing from 12 to 8 teams, seeds were sown from which serious rivalry would sprout.

Many cities had their teams abandon them. A shift in growth to the west would also come into play. Other places could now support a team. The birth of the American League was a slow and steady process as they worked toward major league status.

143

It defiantly arrived in 1901 as a self-described equal to the National League. It would have a profound impact on shaping the destiny of major league baseball throughout the 20th century.

Byron Bancroft "Ban" Johnson was a young Cincinnati sports scribe who cherished baseball but hated its immoral insolence. In his articles, Johnson aggressively crusaded for a clean game where players behaved, umpires were in control, and rowdy patrons were thrown out of the ballpark. Charles Comiskey, an effective player-manager in the majors since age 23, challenged him to make good on his complaints by getting involved.

Ban Johnson cut his teeth in the Western League, to start. He had a policy of fair and clean play. Under his leadership, the league became a critical and financial hit. It didn't go unnoticed by the National League magnates but was shrugged off and considered insignificant at the time.

In 1900 Ban Johnson fired two warning shots across the National League's bow, renaming his league the American League and moving Comiskey to Chicago. The National League was okay with the move so long as the Chicago club played in the gritty industrial south side of the "windy city" and did not use the name "Chicago" in any of its identifiers. Hence the team was only known as the "White Stockings" Initially, Johnson was happy to be in the backyard of major league baseball. Johnson was about to let all the fur fly with the National Agreement on Baseball and minor leagues about to expire.

In 1901, Johnson removed the kid gloves and went for the kill. He moved league teams into the abandoned National League cities of Baltimore and Washington and added teams in Detroit, Milwaukee, and Cleveland, along with the afore to

144

mentioned Chicago. Next came the unexpected. He moved teams into Philadelphia and Boston, two National League strongholds. A hostile full-scale interleague war replaced any goodwill gestures by the National League.

After signing National League players for above the $2400 maximum, the war was on. In the end, the American League held its own. Their attendance averaged 3,100 as opposed to 3,500 in the National League. In the cities where the two leagues competed, the results were mixed. In both Chicago and Boston, the American Leaguers outdrew the National Leaguers two to one. Only in Philadelphia did the Phillies have more fans attend than the Athletics, but only barely.

Be that as it may, our focus is on how this affected the Ebbets team in Brooklyn. Unfortunately for Ebbets, along with the fans, the loss of a pitching ace, a starting infielder, and an outfielder was just the beginning of the American League hijacking of players. In 1902 the Superbas also lost two .300 hitters and hall of fame pitcher Joe Kelley. It appears that 1903 was the last year Gus Abell put any more money into the team, leaving Ebbets with a beer budget at best. Ebbets had no war chest, and on account of that, the team slowly sank into the second division. 5th through 7th place in an eight-team league seemed to be their yearly fate for the rest of the decade. For some reason, the Pittsburg team went un-raided and finished in first place for three straight years (1901-1902-1903). The New York Giants and Chicago Cubs mostly won for the rest of the decade. In Ned Hanlon's last few years as manager of the Brooklyn team, he kept player-poor teams in contention to his credit. But beginning in 1904, with no more Gus Abell backing, even Hanlon could not stop the bloodletting that lack of capital and

145

players caused. Not surprisingly, Hanlon left to manage Cincinnati for two years finishing sixth each time.

In January 1903, the National and American Leagues met in Cincinnati to make peace. It was the number one priority. The key points were mutual recognition and keeping the reserve clause intact. Players' contracts and scheduling were also of importance. Cities needed to have two teams that are not playing home games at the same time so as not to compete for patrons' dollars. The magnates all agreed to this as it was self-serving.

Most of the magnates were not concerned about the New York Market. The Baltimore Orioles (the second iteration of that name) played in the American League for the 1901 and 1902 seasons. In 1903 the Baltimore Orioles moved to New York and assumed the appellation "Highlanders." The Giants and Dodgers were not pleased but wanted peace. They seemed unconcerned if the new team moved too far away from Manhattan. Ebbets understood the benefits of the peace agreement. The two-year war with the American League gutted his championship team. While the Highlander club initially was unsuccessful in playing at Hilltop Park from 1903-1912, they moved to the Giants Polo Grounds Park in 1913. They then changed their name to the New York Yankees. Beer Magnate Jake Rupert bought the team in 1915 and started infusing the team with beer profits, building Yankee Stadium in 1922. Ebbets had no idea he would have to contend with such an alcoholic money-making machine in future years. Few did!

The feud continued, however, as the Highlanders started scheduling Sunday Games at nearby Ridgewood Park in Queens. There was no ban on doing so in the agreement between the two leagues, so the Highlanders felt they were justified. The lack of Sunday games had cost the Brooklyn Team plenty of money over the years, but Queens County had no such blue laws. Past Brooklyn teams had played there before and made some money. Brooklyn felt their territorial rights were being violated. It took the slow machinations of the two leagues time to settle the matter, but eventually, Brooklyn prevailed. If Sunday games were allowed, Brooklyn would have made a hefty profit, so Ebbets got tricky and tried several ploys. The first was free admission while paying the ticket price for a program. That worked but eventually was defeated. His next ploy was letting the public pay through donations. Again, this was defeated through legal channels. You can't deny his very creative ploys were, at the very least amusing.

Bancroft and his Baseball Hall of Fame plaque.

CHAPTER NINETEEN
The Building of Ebbets Field

At the end of 1908, the 10-year lease at Washington Park II was about to expire. A decision had to be made before the Spring of 1909 on what to do. Charles Ebbets was not about to repeat the experience of building a new ballpark and finding the land on such short notice. The building of Washington Park II had given him perspective. He intimately knew all the downsides of doing such a venture. A steel and cement ballpark would provide different challenges that didn't exist with a wooden ballpark. This time Ebbets wanted to own the land and not pay exorbitant rent. He was in a bind as the new season would begin in about half a year. Moving was on his mind, but that had to wait for another day. Ebbets decided to sign a five-year lease with no option for the 1913 season at Washington Park. If a move was going to be made, it should happen by the Spring of 1913 at the latest.

In June of 1909, Ebbets made an off-hand comment that nobody seemed to pick up on the land where a new park would be placed before 1913. The first plot of land had already been purchased by September 1908. It had been determined that the new generation of parks would be of the steel-brick-cement variety. Wood wasn't cutting edge, and there was always the specter of fires associated with it.

In 1911, there were rumors about the club returning to the Eastern Park area in Brownsville, East New York. The game plan had already been decided, but this rumor and others were purposely used as a smokescreen.

Charles Ebbets fought with everyone over money matters and no longer had Gus Abell as a war chest. Ball players' salaries were cut, and he grudgingly had to pay a player an increase. Charlie bickered with sporting goods manufacturers over the price of bats, balls, gloves, and uniforms. Every penny taken at the gate was micromanaged. Employees were lectured about being economical, and small bills were refused or delayed. The land was bought in small parcels for his new ballpark with any spare cash that could be found or saved. Ebbets appeared to be hell-bent on making it to the debtor's prison. Everyone saw what was happening. None knew why.

Ebbets first thought was to buy the Litchfield land that Washington Park was located on and build a new park there. The feeling was that the grandstand could be moved from Fourth Avenue to Third Avenue, making it bigger and adding more bleachers. The entirety of Washington Park would have to be removed and disposed of, which was no small task! It would be a very costly operation. On second thought, it was decided to ditch that plan and find a new place. With that in mind, Charlie started exploring various parts of Brooklyn, looking for available land. At times it had to be done on foot. Neighborhoods, growth patterns, transportation facilities, maps, and plans for service by the Brooklyn Rapid Transportation

Company were analyzed. The final idea was to put the new park in Flatbush, about two and a half miles from the former Washington Park sites in South Brooklyn. There were various ways to get to the new location using eight main trolley lines, and the Brighton Beach "L" (elevated train line) 38 transfer points were also available.

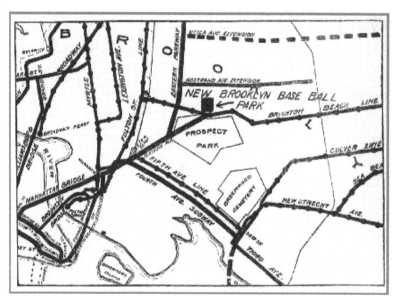

Various train and trolley lines to get to Ebbets Field

Ebbets did his homework. The new location was less than half the distance to the former East New York site. The situation was very well understood as he later told his daughter Lydie Mae "if you live long enough, you'll live to see Ebbets Field in the heart of Brooklyn, and someday the park will be too small," and the team would have to move. Considering that event was some 44 years later, Charles H. Ebbets was prescient. In a world of trolley cars and elevated trains, how could one foresee a future of vehicles, parking lots, and superhighways? Transportation and baseball were in their embryonic stages. Ebbets commented at a league banquet that was delivered as an expression of faith that became famous in the annals of sport. That quote was that "Baseball is still in its "infancy" His fellow magnates, who generally saw no more than 10,000 fans for weekend games, all rolled on the floor convulsed in mirth. The rejoinder was, "it's a pretty old baby Charlie."

The land found was not very attractive to the eye. Squatters lived there. In the middle was a giant hole where those living in the shanties dumped their garbage. This ramshackle, seedy neighborhood was saddled with the moniker "Pigtown." The supposed land was slightly under 5 acres in size and bordered by Bedford Avenue, Sullivan Street, Montgomery Street, and Franklin Avenue. He never got the land between Franklin Street and Cedar Streets, and Cedar Street was renamed Mc Keever Place in 1932 after two future co-owners of the park.

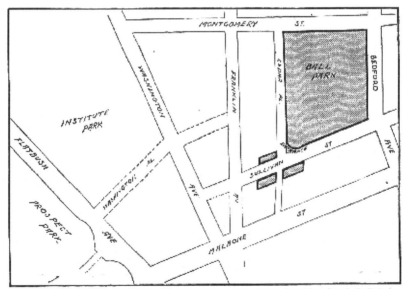

Tint Shows Property in Flatbush Bought by the Owners of the Brooklyn Baseball Club for the Erection of a Great New Ball Park.

In his vision was seen all the land filled and leveled with a new state-of-the-art field put right in the middle. He brought his friends to see this fantastic new site. They only saw a craggy huddle of dilapidated shacks surrounding a hole in the ground. It had an odorous, steaming stench of decomposing garbage coming out of the earth. His friends unanimously told him that he was crazy, foolish, unwise, irrational, or just plain "nuts." They also told him he was too far from South Brooklyn; Park Slope; Brooklyn Heights; Williamsburg; Greenpoint, or Gowanus. Erstwhile he found no enthusiasm or support from these friends.

Charles Ebbets ignored their sentiments as people of vision are wont to do and began researching the site. Thirty-odd parcels owned by either deeds or squatters' rights were found. Both his attorney Bernard J. York and his real Estate agent Howard Pyle recommended secrecy. They wisely felt that if announced, the price would go up. A "shell" corporation was founded with the appellation of the Pylon Construction Company to hide its actual purposes. Unfortunately, and coincidentally, the Real Estate company that oversaw the purchase had the name "C. Pyle & Company." Purchasing parcels of land was begun. Landowners seeing the similarity between the two names (Pyle and Pylon), assumed some big land corporation was buying the land to develop. It added to the sellers asking price. Had they known the truth, the asking price might have been even higher. Land costs $200,000 (half in cash, half in notes). The only note Ebbets had in place was a $100,000 two-year loan from the Mechanics Bank In New York. Former team owner George Chauncey was president of this bank.

Ebbets needed budget land as his bank account woefully indicated that nothing else could be afforded. It never would get done without generous amounts of snake oil and mirrors. The field was yet to be built and was estimated to cost $750,000, equal to about $2,000,000 today. There was no money left.

There are two versions of the story of how the last piece of land was purchased. Ebbets had to have this last piece or could not finish anything. The owner of this land went to Berlin (or the Alps) and then to Paris (or not). From there, the trail went cold. Later the landholder was found in California (all accounts) and left (or not). Supposedly the owner went to Montclair, New Jersey (or stayed in California). Finally, he was delighted to find out that someone was interested in his land and sold it for $500 or suspected that it must be worth more with all the hoopla. $2000 was asked for and received. No wonder in the state of human affairs, we have legends and myths given this story.

"Pigtown," Future home of Ebbets Field in Flatbush

Just after Christmas in 1911, Charles Ebbets sent out an invitation for dinner at 129 Pierrepont Street on January 2, 1912. Something was up. Part of the invitation was in red ink and read "a very important piece of news" was to be announced. Ebbets was about to unspring the news of his carefully guarded plans to the public.

Brooklyn had four essential papers at the time, so the invitees included their Sports Writers: Abe Yager of the *Brooklyn Eagle*; Leonard Wooster of the *Brooklyn Times*; William Granger of *the Citizen*, and William Rafter of the *Standard-Times*. Not to miss out on the national audience Damon Runyan and Grantland Rice were also included. As cheap as Ebbets usually was, he left out no embellishment for this earth-shaking news announcement. A "bounteous repast" was included, and each attendee was given a solid silver cigarette case commemorating the event. While the ice cream was being served, Ebbets served up the fact that Brooklyn was about to have a new state-of-the-art ballpark. The announcement was like a bomb being set off and was met with rousing applause.

From the original plans, we see a proposed 30,000-seat park which included a centerfield bleacher section that wasn't built. The final number of seats was 24,000.

The most Ebbets Field ever held in its history was some 35,000 seats. It was considered a "bandbox" by many in its later years. Right field was considered too close as Bedford Avenue got in the way. Hindsight says that more land directly across the street should have been purchased so that more fans could have been seated in right field in future years. History tells us that funny bounces off the cement would never have happened.

There would have been no Dixie Walker or Carl Furillo "The Reading Rifle" playing caroms off the wall and saving Abe Stark from having to buy a suit every time the "Hit Sign, Win Suit" was dinged. The sign was only hit twice, both by Mel Ott of the Giants. Abe Stark became Brooklyn Borough president because of this ploy. History was more fun!

Ebbets Field was nearing completion in 1913. Note that no one lived there at this time.

At the groundbreaking ceremonies, the site was described as containing several old houses, shanties, goats, and tomato cans, and the streets bordering the field were mapped out. Two of them, Montgomery, and Sullivan (named after two of George Washington's generals from the revolutionary war), had not even been built yet.

There was one last detail to complete, and that was named the park. Ebbets was coy and suggested calling it Washington Park again. It was pointed out to him that this name was inappropriate because the new location was nowhere near the Battle of Brooklyn site. Ebbets suggested that the four Brooklyn Newspapers decide on the name. They bandied it about figuring out that since the new park was Charles Ebbet's baby, he would sink or swim with the consequences. They decided it should be named after him. Maybe he wanted to do so anyway but did not have the temerity to make such a self-serving decision. Leonard Wooster of the Brooklyn Times made the final suggestion, and Ebbets agreed. Hence the name "Ebbets Field."

Construction began on March 4, 1912, with the cornerstone, a piece of Connecticut granite that held newspapers, pictures of baseball players, cards, telegrams, and almanacs, was laid on July 6, 1912. At the cornerstone-laying ceremony, Ebbets said that the ballpark would be ready for play on September 1, 1912, and that Brooklyn would win the National League pennant in 1913. Neither event proved true.

Demonstrating that the press can be a two-sided sword, Ebbets invited them to see his new site. They unanimously saw what Ebbets friends noticed, but unfortunately, they got to write about it.

Sports scribe York labeled the hole in the middle as "the subway to China" Tom Rice from the *Brooklyn Eagle* advised that if one were to go, they should bring a cane and a walking stick. He went on to further describe the locale as "pleasantly diversified" with "rambling and picturesque homes of squatters" close to and in an "amateur section of the Grand Canyon." (his version of the subway to China) Still seeking adjectives and adverbs to assault nouns, Rice described the streets as models of what streets should not be. He called it "walking through mud on the way to a lot more mud." Rice was prophetic, though, in saying that the land preparation would be both timely and costly. It was not going to be a cakewalk like Washington Park II was. That land was flat and level.

Seeing this site in "Pigtown" as a future ballpark took a lot of imagination. It also took a lot more money than Ebbets had.

He would have to find "a genie in a lamp" or the "goose that laid golden eggs" or some permutation. In the mix was the variability of the weather. If one were to look at the newspapers of January and February of 1912, headlines of violent cold weather that froze tugboats in the East River would be seen. Oystermen were unable to get to their potential catch as well. Due to this, the future site of Ebbets field was frozen down to 38 inches. No construction would begin until March 4, 1912.

Ebbets and his architect Clarence Van Buskirk spent time visiting other ballparks to make sure that mistakes seen there were not repeated at his new park. Some innovations included an 80-foot rotunda suggested by Charles H. Ebbets at the main entrance for ticket sales. It had a chandelier with baseballs hanging and a white marble baseball embedded in the floor.

Ebbets Field Rotunda

Other novelties included a Central Indicator Station with a megaphone to announce game changes. Public Telephones were also added. Diverse entrances for different classes of seats made ingress and egress easier. This wasn't seen in some of the other ballparks Ebbets, and Van Buskirk visited. These entrances were tested to the maximum when the park first opened, and some tweaks still had to be made.

Ebbets finally admitted that he bit off more than he could chew and had to find help completing his project. He was broke. Perhaps he could have gotten a thirty-year mortgage. History shows that did not happen.

CHAPTER TWENTY
Steve and Ed McKeever Arrive

In August of 1912, Charlie Ebbets and his financial troubles were finally alleviated. Bernard J. York, Ebbets lawyer, knew Ed McKeever and introduced the two. Other stories claim they had already known each other since 1883, which was likely since they all swam around in the same political waters.

Steve and Ed McKeever

In any event, the three were or would become very close friends. Steve McKeever, however, felt no affinity for the triumvirate. Later this would prove to be a major schism in the club that would not end until 1937.

Ebbets first had to purchase the stock from his old Brooklyn friend, furniture dealer Henry J. Medicus who helped buy out former owners Harry von Der Horst and Ned Hanlon. Medicus and Ebbets were old bowling league friends. Medicus never meddled in the club's affairs and had no idea about the proposed park in "Pigtown."

Ebbets needed these shares so he could sell a half interest to the McKeevers. Medicus was amenable as he only wanted to help his bowling buddy. Ebbets now owned all the club's stock save those owned by his son Charles Jr. He tried at first to get a loan through the McKeevers for $300,000, but the McKeevers wanted part ownership in the team. Two separate Corporations were formed: the Ebbets-McKeever Exhibition company with Edward J. McKeever as President, Steven W. McKeever as Vice President, Ebbets Sr. as Treasurer, and Ebbets Jr. as secretary. This corporation owned the land and the stands of Ebbets Field. The other corporation was the Brooklyn National League Club, with Ebbets Sr. as president, Ed McKeever as Vice President, Steve McKeever as treasurer, and Ebbets Jr. as secretary owned the team.

Steve McKeever was the older brother by four years, born in 1859. Ed McKeever was born in 1863. Their father was a cobbler. Both received minimal education. Steve unsuccessfully ran away to become a Civil War drummer boy for the Northern Army. He returned to be employed as a horse boy on a trolley line near the Fulton Street Ferry. He eventually became an apprenticed plumber. One of his first jobs was doing plumbing work on the Brooklyn Bridge. Ed worked for a brass fitter, following which he started the "Hudson River Broken Stone Company" along with a friend Michael J. Daly. Within a few years, the McKeever brothers formed the E. J. & S.W. McKeever Contracting Company combining their expertise in plumbing and stonework. Both loved and played baseball in their youth. Steve played second base and was captain of the old Brooklyn Eagles team. Ed played shortstop and was captain of the Blue Lights team. Both were fans of the Atlantic's team that ended the Cincinnati Red Stockings' winning streak. They watched and played in the shadows of the pylons that became the Brooklyn Bridge. Baseball had them hooked.

The McKeevers acquired a knack for making money from lessons learned while doing endless jobs too long to list other than those previously mentioned. Wealth was acquired at a relatively young age. Trying and failing to get various Brooklyn City contracts was complex, even if they were the low bidders. The contract the brothers finally were awarded was for the removal of dead animals from the streets of Brooklyn. They almost lost that contract because they did not have a plant to process the animal's remains. Finally, a processing plant on the Barren Islands (which later became Floyd Bennett Field by pumping in sand from Jamaica Bay as fill) was purchased for $100,000 that should have only cost $25,000. The prior owners knew they had them over a barrel. Despite this early encumbrance, the business was sold in 1910 sold for $1,000,000. It was shortly before Ebbets Field was built. The McKeevers were now flush with fresh capital to spend as they wished.

In their litany of jobs, two would be crucial to the project being shared with Charles H. Ebbets. One was where the miles

161

of sewer was laid along with granite and asphalt pavements. The other was a plant built to make reinforced concrete. At one point, they also quarried, crushed, and furnished all the ballast rock for the New York Central Railroad between New York City and Buffalo, New York.

If that weren't enough, the McKeever brothers went into general contracting and erected over 1000 homes in Greenpoint, Brooklyn, in one season. The area was called "McKeeverville". They had the ability to construct Ebbets Field. Such a project would be a cakewalk, given their backgrounds. Ebbets only needed to sit back and provide the plans. The McKeevers would do the rest. Ebbets was too hands-on to play that role, however. They were sure the new park would be highly profitable and were quite willing to give Charlie the help he needed in anticipation of sharing the profits. None of this overextended their enormous wealth.

Ed was quiet and reticent. In all his years as an officer of the club, very few got to know him as that was not his nature. Steve was quite the opposite. He had a free and easy way about him. Daily he could be seen with his derby, gold watch, and diamond stickpin. Steve McKeever had a rolling gait and carried a blackthorn stick. He was called "Judge," and everybody he met was addressed as "Judge." He would often ask, "How are your wife and kids, Judge?" If you told him, you didn't have any, he became distraught. He believed firmly that all men should have a wife and kids and that a wife was meant to be for eternity. He was a devout, inflexible Roman Catholic. The Ebbets family came from a Dutch Reformed background, and both Charlie (1923) and one of his daughters Lydie Mae (1914), divorced. The "Judge" became incensed over the situation, judging them as bad people. Steve McKeever hated the Ebbets family. After the death of Charlie and Ed McKeever (within one week of each other) some dozen years later, he wreaked havoc on the organization. It did not end until 1937, when the Brooklyn National Trust Company (which had taken over George Chauncey's Mechanics bank loan) took over the club's running and hired Larry MacPhail to get the team back on a positive cash flow basis. Larry did so, wipe out the debt, and paid off most of the Equitable Life mortgage within four years.

In any event, all the commotion in getting this done took its toll on Charlie Ebbet's health, and by his doctor's orders, he took a relaxing cruise to New Orleans, where he could rest and take the team's thoughts off his mind. He had done all he could and had to address his own human frailties. The alternative was a nervous breakdown.

Ebbets was writing a history of baseball in Brooklyn at the time along with Tom Rice of the *Brooklyn Eagle* from January through March 11, 1912, which abruptly ended. Near the end, many days were skipped without advance notice, even though each story ended with the caveat of "to be continued tomorrow." At the field level, the floor of the Rotunda was unfinished. Various paving projects were also left incomplete. Unwillingly, Ebbets dropped everything and left the finishing work to his son Charles Jr. and the McKeevers. When he returned to Brooklyn's, the new ballpark was ready for its' grand opening. It wound up like a scene out of a classic Marx brothers' comedy.

Ebbets Field as seen from Montgomery Street in 1913

CHAPTER TWENTY-ONE
Opening Daze

Consternation was frozen on the faces of Charles Ebbets and the McKeevers as they awaited the opening day of their state-of-the-art ballpark. The weather was always of concern in early April in Brooklyn.

To get this far, they had to find their way through the perplexing ownership web of the National League. Each team postured for what was good for them. Celebrating the opening of Ebbets Field was not a priority for the other magnates. Finally, after all the gyrations, the Brooklyn team was able to schedule an exhibition game with a rival American League team known as the New York Yankees. It was not yet the team remade by Jake Rupert's beer money. That wouldn't happen until a few years later. In 1913 the Yankees began sharing the Polo Grounds with the Giants and would not build Yankee Stadium until 1922.

Anyone interested in Sports Journalism should find copies of all the local newspapers and read their imaginative, colorful, capricious, ingenious, lively, flamboyant, inventive, impulsive, whimsical, and quirky reporting. It was a perfect time for them to launch salvos of adjectives and adverbs at unsuspecting nouns and verbs. After all, their job could very well depend on their aerial bombardments from Noah Webster.

Model T Ford flies by Ebbets Field in 1913

Anyone interested in Sports Journalism should find copies oIt was a time when radio and television did not exist. Information had to be passed along by the written word. Many families received four or more weekly newspapers to read alternative versions of stories. With baseball, these scribes had to paint pictures that the reader could visualize. There were fans of various reporters. In many cases, there was more than one favorite. It was not a world of "instant replays" in slow motion that spoke for themselves.

Concern was noted about the weather, given reports of overnight rain. The momentous day turned out just fine and was described as "one of the nicest little spring days that the oldest residents could remember" Apparently, the residents of "Pigtown" had quite a fine "cherce" of over "toity" words. They even went there and "seened" it for themselves.

The ballpark was going to be tested, as was the mass transportation system web connected to it. Ebbets must have also hired Mack Sennett and his "Keystone Cops" to oversee the festivities. Remember that in the recent past, a journey to the park was described as a jaunt through the mud on the way to more mud! The trolleys and trains were taxed to the maximum, with an estimated over 10,000 people crossing the East River. Patrons were "bumped and bruised" like pears on the way to market. The Brighton and Fulton elevated train lines "fairly groaned with crowds" as if experiencing pain through their non-existent nervous systems. Perhaps they put more "earl" on their wheel bearings for lubrication due to the excess weight. The trolleys were not to be left out of the ordeal with their over-crowded, overweight steerage compartments as they carried "their share of eager fans." The convenience of trains and trollies turned inconvenient.

In 1913 automobiles were still rare but were also part of the ornate cacophony of verbiage. The entourage of cars was described as "the most elaborate motor display ever seen on this side of the river." An erudite resident rejoined that "there ain't that many machines made"

No matter how people got to Ebbets Field, the "hurrying, chatty and happy" horde arrived at "the gates which open into the handsome lobby of the stadium." (Rotunda) When the gates opened, New York harbor had a rival for high and low tides. Over 150 police were on hand and had to alternately open and close the 80-foot Rotunda, which immediately became a huge bottleneck. As tickets were purchased, the next wave was allowed in. It continued for quite some time. The turnstiles were described as "sluice gates of a dam." The crowd got to see for the first time the benefit of ramps versus stairways. These ramps were not seen at Washington Park II.

Scribes anticipated that once the initial crowd had their first experience with the field, there would be quotable verbosity for their gristmill of words. It proved to be true. There were "hearty shouts of approval" with their "first sweeping glance of Ebbets great new plant." Few would forget their initial experience at the field. They quickly claimed it was "a wonder and no mistake." The business of the city was summarily set aside shortly after noon," even though Saturday was usually a workday. The people of Brooklyn wanted to celebrate the occasion.

Ebbets only regret was that his 24,000-seat stadium could not accommodate an additional 10,000 fans. It was a similar problem that Walter O'Malley would face 40 years later. The fans were not to be left out and, like a frontiersman, sought out alternative viewing options. There was a high point just across Montgomery Street where the famous Crow Hill Penitentiary was formerly located. Here a partial view could be gotten for free. Since we are a country of budding entrepreneurs, amateur builders manufactured rickety stands that could hold up to "300 or more". This graphically shows why "fans" is short for "fanatics." Any fractional view was sought out, whether it be "houses, barns, trees and telegraph poles," or the "few trees bent under a load of boys and men."

Some others risked "breaking their necks to get a peek at the players from a distance of two city blocks." Any other possible vantage point was sought out.

We still have not gotten to the celebratory opening or the game! That almost seemed a side story to the crowd and their antics. Charlie Chaplin would have approved.

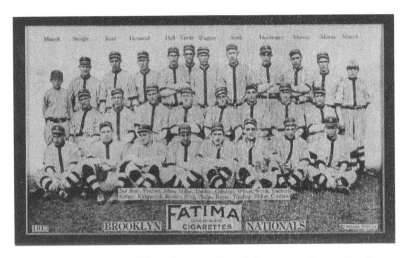

1913 Fatima Brooklyn Team Card from authors Dodger Museum collection

The game time was set for 3:00 PM. Now it was time for the owners to add to the circus-like atmosphere. As the proceedings began, Ebbets walked to the flagpole with Ed and Jenny McKeever to start the flag-raising ceremony. Unfortunately, no one brought the flag, which was left back in Ebbets' office. This event almost seemed like Groucho Marx and his brothers in "Horsefeathers" trying to leave a boat with the stolen passport of Maurice Chevalier. The start of the game was delayed a half-hour with the raising of the misplaced flag. Shannon's Band played the "Star-Spangled Banner," and Genevieve Ebbets (Charlie's youngest daughter) threw out the first ball. Thankfully she wasn't given one of her dad's bowling balls by mistake.

The game almost seemed like a sideline to all the festivities and merriment but fortunately went quickly. Since the actual contestation did not start until after 3:30 PM, it might have ended due to a lack of light which, given everything else, would have been a fitting ending. Even so, this almost happened. Brooklyn had a two-run lead going into the ninth inning due to two inside-the-park home runs by rookie Casey Stengel and first baseman Jake Daubert. As would be typical of a W. C. Fields movie, Brooklyn pitcher Frank Allen threw the ball away, allowing the Yankees to tie the score in the top of the ninth. It set the stage for a dramatic ending from a "Flash Gordon" cliffhanger. Future hall of famer Zach Wheat was driven home by Carlisle Smith in the bottom of the ninth for a walk-off victory. It capped off a perfect day. The Yankees and Casey Stengel would be back in future years, but that is another day's narration. One might think that the story ended here, but the lightning ending left fans trying to figure out how to get out of Ebbets Field, which generated "no little commotion." Special police and firemen had to come to the aid of the fans.

Hall of Famers Casey Stengel (left), Zach Wheat (right)

No new ballpark was devoid of glitches. The biggest problems were too few entrances and ticket lines keeping people who had already bought tickets from entering the park. The 80-foot Rotunda was too small. Shortly thereafter, Ebbets remedied the situation by adding four new ticket entrances and allowing an exit point in the centerfield. There would be a lot more drama in the 44 years of life the park had left. It would have a dramatic, unexpected ending. But at least for that day, everybody went home happy.

Ed McKeever, Charles H. Ebbets as Genevieve Ebbets throws out the first ball.

CHAPTER TWENTY-TWO
Washington Park Three and the War with the Federal League (1914-1915)

Charles Ebbets had seen his share of baseball wars. Just as he started with the team, there was the Union Association war in 1884 that lasted one year. He saw the results of the Players League and the move to Eastern Park firsthand in 1891 as an assistant secretary. In the war with the American League, he saw players raided from his championship team and taken away to the point where his team was a non-contender. Ebbets claimed that the new league really wasn't a threat but acknowledged that the previous wars taught him to "never underestimate the enemy." He realized that a better way was needed for a more structured relationship with the players. If not, more of these rebellions were likely to happen. Now out of the blue, another new league reared its ugly head.

172

March 8, 1913, the Federal League was born in Indianapolis, Indiana, just as Ebbets Field was about to open. John Powers, who earlier had tried to establish another major league called the "Colombian League," was elected president of the infant circuit. Unlike the American and National Leagues, the Federal League did not plan to be part of the National Commission of baseball and follow its rules. Instead, it wished to be independent. At the time, it intended no player raids against the established leagues but would develop its own players as an alternative.

Initially, it was only able to establish six teams in its premier season. The cities represented were Chicago, Cincinnati, Cleveland, Indianapolis, Pittsburgh, and St. Louis. This would put the Federal League into competition with five major league cities and one minor league market. (Indianapolis) The Federal League vowed not to interfere with organized baseball but, rather, would only sign theoretical "free agents." Unfortunately, what organized baseball and the Federal League considered "free agents" differed due to the infamous "reserve clause." known as Rule 10 A, which stated: "On or before January 15, the Club may tender to the Player a contract for the term of that year by mailing the same to the Player. If prior to the March 1 next succeeding said January 15, the Player and the Club have not agreed upon the terms of such contract, then on or before 10 days after said March 1, the Club shall have the right to renew this contract for the period of one year."

A team was added by the Federal League in Brooklyn, which was purchased by the bakery magnate Robert Ward of Ward Brother's bakeries, who promptly baptized the team and gave it the moniker of the "Brooklyn Tip Tops," after their bread. Apparently, former Brooklyn team owner Ned Hanlon

173

pushed Ward to start a team in Brooklyn as some modicum of revenge for "Foxy Ned's" untimely leaving.

The new Brooklyn Federal Club caused such a controversy in the New York and Brooklyn media that Ward renamed his franchise the "Brookfeds." This ploy circumvented the usage of "Brooklyn" as an identifier. The Wards proposed to Charles Ebbets a series between their respective teams, which was met with about as much enthusiasm as a Federal League/World Series championship tournament did. What was truly unique was that Ward went back to the original Washington Park 2 site and constructed a steel-cement-brick ballpark. Ebbets had considered doing the same thing as well but decided to move to Flatbush instead. No doubt Ebbets would have to compete for fans and money with a new ballpark within 3 miles of Ebbets Field.

Washington Park III, home of the "Brookfeds" ball club

In 1914 it was estimated that the attendance at Washington Park III was 77,000. Only 122,671 patrons visited Ebbets Field (a decrease of 64%). Ebbets lost $54,000, while Ward lost over $85,000. Nobody won this battle. In 1915 the tides totally turned so that the attendance at Ebbets Field doubled, reaching 300,000 (an estimated $68,000 profit), while hardly anyone visited Washington Park.

However, the fickle finger of fate stepped in when Robert Ward, the wealthy owner of the Brooklyn Tip Tops, passed away

174

in the fall of 1915. Much of the fight, spirit, and vision of the Federal league died with him.

Robert Ward, owner of Tip-Top bread and the Brooklyn Tip-Top baseball team

In the waning days of 1915, attendance was miserable because of the effects of World War 1. The war also worked a hardship on organized baseball as well, but they were better able to handle the stormy days ahead. Even lowering ticket prices in several Federal League cities couldn't bolster attendance. That, coupled with the hefty contracts that the league handed out, spelled doom for the nascent league.

Brookfeds of Federal League at Washington Park III

None of this should be dismissed as insignificant history. What the Federal League did had a seismic impact that would be challenged. Baseball's special antitrust exemption sprang directly from the suit that was hurled by the Baltimore Federal League club against organized baseball.

The suit was presented before the court of Kenesaw Mountain Landis between 1914 and 1915 and was never decided. The Federal League dropped the suit as part of a "peace agreement." Landis deliberately delayed the ruling on the matter anyway. Landis was a baseball fan himself, and in the trial transcripts, Landis said to the Federal League attorneys: "Do you realize that a decision, in this case, may tear down the very foundations of this game so loved by thousands"?

He realized that baseball was in violation of antitrust laws but was reticent to issue a ruling in the matter. This was a massive break for organized baseball because of Landis' reputation as a "trust buster." In the future, Baseball returned the favor that Landis did for them. They made Judge Landis baseball's first commissioner of baseball. This was after the wake of the notorious Chicago Black Sox Scandal, where the Sox threw the 1919 World Series.

Kenesaw Mountain Landis and His Baseball Hall of Fame Plaque

Regarding wars with other leagues, there would only be one more left in Baseball History. The Continental League of Professional Baseball was proposed as a third major league for baseball in the United States and Canada. The Continental League was an idea of attorney William Shea who first proposed it in November of 1958. On July 27, 1959, the new Continental League was officially announced. Former Dodgers president Branch Rickey was named as the league president. On August 18, 1959. Appearing as a guest on the live CBS broadcast of "What's My Line" on Sunday, September 13, 1959, he pronounced the new league as "Inevitable as tomorrow morning." On February 18, 1960, Rickey announced an opening date of April 18, 1961. They were scheduled to begin to play in the 1961 season. Unlike previous leagues such as the Players' League and the Federal League, it sought membership within baseball's existing organization and acceptance by Major League Baseball. The league disbanded in August 1960 without ever playing a single game. This was a concession by William A. Shea (of Shea Stadium fame) as part of his negotiations with Major League Baseball. They wanted to expand and incorporate at least eight new cities. The United States population was expanding west, and of the eight proposed Continental League cities, all but one would eventually receive relocated or expansion of Major League Baseball franchises. They included Minneapolis–St. Paul in 1961, Houston and New York in 1962, Atlanta in 1966, Dallas/Ft. Worth in 1972, Toronto in 1977, and Denver in 1993. Buffalo was the only one of the proposed expansion teams to never happen. Just as America itself started with 13 colonies, all on the east coast, the American and National leagues had 16 teams, all located east of St. Louis and North of Washington D.C. Both followed their manifest destiny to fill their borders from sea to shining sea. This, in both cases, is truly an American story.

The "Mahatma" Branch Rickey Continental League President

CHAPTER TWENTY-THREE
The Wall and Snack Bar Controversies

There remains some controversy regarding the remains of Washington Park itself. One essential picture is necessary to determine the answer. There is still a brick wall that partially stands as either part of Ebbets Washington Park 2 or Wards Washington Park 3. If it were Ebbets Washington Park II, it would precede both Fenway Park (1912) and Wrigley Field (1914) as the oldest standing wall of any major league park. There are arguments on both sides.

Washington Park 2 or 3? The controversy is about the windowed section on the right.

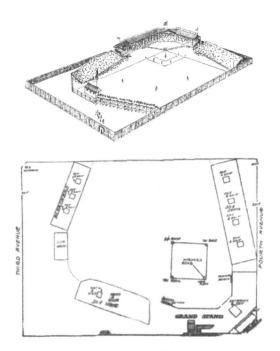

The controversy concerns the Third Avenue wall on the left of both illustrations.

Was the windowed wall in the middle pre-Washington Park III?

The dispute seems to rely on the following questions: Why would you build the wall before anything else? Why would the wall be started before demolition ended? Why would the wall suddenly change style? Why would it be taller on the left? Why were the bricks on the left lighter than those on the right? Lastly, why would you put windows in a stadium wall?" The picture's windowed wall to the left is argued to be older than the parapet walls to the right. It predates the 1914 construction by the Tip Tops.

All these are valid points of contention. Without a higher quality 1914 view of the corner of First Street and Third Avenue, there is no complete proof. That may be where the story remains stalled.

Part of the Washington Park Wall was removed in 2010

The site was visited and searched. The Consolidated Edison people were accommodating and kind. They could add no fuel to either fire.

Close-Up Controversial Wall Section

A manager said he wanted to show something he never spoke to anyone about. Meandering around several bends, he came to a roll-up window. When the window was rolled up, spools of wire were behind it. He mentioned that as a longtime employee, he was struck by something odd whenever he visited this room. It first happened when the Consolidated Edison Electric Company (Con-Ed) took over the building. He knew the ballpark stories and finally concluded after some deliberation that this was the original refreshment bar of the park. Food and beverages were sold over the counter. To him, the layout could mean nothing else.

Knowing that Coney Island was about 9 miles away, it may be that "hot dogs" were sold here for the first time at a baseball game. Charles Feltman, a Coney Island pie-wagon vendor, sees credit with serving hot dachshund sausages on milk rolls as early as 1867. The National Hot Dog and Sausage Council claim that Feltman opened a hot dog stand on Coney Island in 1871 and sold 3,684 sausages that year. The business was booming until Nathan Handwerker, a bread slicer at Feltman's, left to open his stand in 1916. He undercut his former boss, charging half the price per dog (five cents instead of ten). Today, Nathan's Famous hot dogs are known universally.

Harry M. Stevens, a British-born Ohioan, is said to be the first to sell sausage-in-a-bun at a New York Giants game in 1901, calling them dachshund dogs. He could not sell ice cream on cold days in April, so he came up with this new "hot" alternative. When a cartoonist covering the event couldn't spell dachshund, the street food's colloquial name was born as he captioned his cartoon "hot dog" after hearing vendors shout, "They're red hot! Get your dachshund sausages while they're red hot!" It would not be surprising that hot dogs made their way to Washington Park by this time and were sold or prepared through this window. Harry M. Stevens was at Charles H. Byrne's funeral in 1898, so apparently, there already was some connection. If Hot Dogs were being sold at the Polo Grounds in 1901, they likely were also sold at Washington Park. We may never know the answer to the Wall or Hot Dog questions. Maybe we should find an Umpire? On second thought, maybe not! Or perhaps we should leave it as part of the legend and lore of baseball, which seems far more fitting.

Original Hot Dog Stand at Washington Park 2?

CHAPTER TWENTY-FOUR
The 1916 World Series

Charles Ebbets sat forlornly at his desk in Ebbets Field, staring out the window at a windy New York snowstorm. He snickered and remembered that his life had some of the same qualities as the storm. In 1915 his team, now known as the Brooklyn Robins (due to the name associated with his manager Wilbert Robinson), had just finished in third place, 10 games behind the Philadelphia Phillies. He just nodded and smiled at some invisible ghosts from the past that came to mind for a few brief moments.

He had just read a copy of the *Sporting News* that predicted that if the "hitting was up to form…" and the "pitching is what it should be…." "Brooklyn appeared to be the best team in the National League ."Since the World Series had started in 1901, his team had failed to make it there for 15 consecutive years. If these muses were correct, then this would be their first trip. He wistfully hoped the scribes were right. Many pitchers had questions. Nap Rucker was at the end of his brilliant career and would contribute little. Future Hall of Famer Rube Marquard had his best years behind him. Larry Cheney would lose his edge late in the 1916 season. On the positive side, Sherry Smith had won 14 and Jack Coombs 15. Ebbets also had "Weezer" Dell, who sounded like he had problems breathing but was a pretty fair pitcher. From the hitting perspective, Casey Stengel and Zack Wheat had an off-year in 1915 but would storm back in 1916. Jake Daubert was near his .300 average self. But would it be enough? Ebbets had no crystal ball but hoped the savants of the *Sporting News* had some connection to a Madame Blavatsky clone.

His chances were enhanced by having Larry Sutton and his uncanny ability to find relatively obscure prospects in the bushes that others seem to have missed. Ebbets tried and failed to find a reliable shortstop. He went with Ivy Olson, who would commit 47 errors. Olson got angry in practice sessions during spring training and became annoyed by an umpire's call in an intra-squad game. He furiously threw sand all over the ump and was ejected. Casey Stengel loved that. Casey had trouble with his bad temper that season as well. Casey was known to throw and kick dirt at umpires later in his career as a manager. The concept of anger management did not exist in that world.

The National League championship in 1916 was probably the pinnacle of Ebbet's 33-year association with the club from 1883 to 1916. He let the team speak for itself and didn't get into the conversation. That would change once World Series time arrived.

The *Brooklyn Eagle* claimed that at the end of the season, Ebbets went through the "most trying period of his entire career" made more problematic by an "almost unbearable" ear problem with which he "was threatened with deafness in one ear."

To add to the festivities was a discourse about World Series ticket prices. In the 1915 World Series, $3 was charged for a reserved seat in the front rows of the upper and lower grandstands. Ebbets decided to raise the ticket price from $3 to

$5. It unleashed the adjective and adverb machine known as the "Press." Fred Lieb of the New York Sun began the festivities by saying that Ebbets "has pulled another bone," claiming that the ticket price was "far in excess of anything ever asked for World Series tickets ."Lieb also reminded the cranks that Ebbets had tried to get the other magnates to agree to eliminate 25-cent seats, charging 50 cents instead. Supposedly the fans were the sheep, and it was Ebbets job to fleece them. Charlie tried to deflect the situation by blaming it on The National Convention of Baseball. It was not true, and his hand in this was more than he would admit. Ever the storyteller, Ebbets claimed that the higher prices were necessary to uphold Brooklyn's' "civic pride," This was because the people of Brooklyn would not want the gate receipts to be embarrassingly low. Lieb's rejoinder was he doubted that the denizens of Brooklyn would lose any sleep over the decision. Ebbets then switched gears and claimed that the club had a right and a responsibility to recover "the tremendous outlay" it took to build a team that made it to the World Series.

Tom Rice of the *Brooklyn Eagle* flip-flopped, taking both sides (aka double talk). At first, he sided with the "indignant yeomanry who arose and called Charles H. Ebbets names." Then Rice switched gears and commented about the "pitifully small attendance" at Ebbets Field. Ebbets did not propose to increase the ticket price for a standard fan's bleacher seat. Fortunately, Ebbets had to leave town for the opening of the 1916 World Series. The last time all this discourse was seen, it was fertilizing a corn field in Nebraska for some 20 years. However, it sold many newspapers justifying Lieb's and Rice's salaries.

On Friday, October 6, 1916, Charles Ebbets left with a convoy of 18 cars and crossed the East River and the Brooklyn Bridge on the way to Grand Central Station. As he meandered through the Brooklyn streets to the bridge, he was met by office workers and fans cheers. Even Brooklyn Trollies stopped in their paths to honor the squire of Brooklyn Baseball. Throughout all this, his ear still hurt.

Some seven hours later, he arrived at the Brunswick Hotel in Boston to begin the festivities.

In the 1915 and 1916 World Series, the Red Sox did not play their home games at Fenway Park. Braves Field held 40,000 fans, far more than Fenway Park, so their home games were held there.

The withering fall verdure of the 1916 season burst for its' final autumnal bloom as both the Robins and Red Sox pursued the last petals of glory as the season was about to end.

Wilbert Robinson started future Hall of Fame pitcher Rube Marquard in the first game. He went up against the 1915 World Series opener and loser Ernie Shore in what initially appeared to be a deadlock. The Red Sox led 2-1 through six innings, with neither pitcher faltering. That ended when both clubs started a scoring frenzy. First, the Red Sox knocked out Rube Marquard for three runs in the seventh. He was taken out and replaced by Jeff Pfeffer, who gave up one more run in the eighth. That run would prove to be the winning run. Brooklyn responded with four runs of their own in the ninth, sending Ernie Shore to the showers. Boston brought in Carl Mays, who stopped the rally and held on for a 6-5 win. It can hardly be said that one team dominated the other. The Red Sox outlasted the Robins. Just a single bounce could have caused a different ending.

**Original 1916 Team Set M 101-4 from author's Dodger
Museum collection**

In game two in Boston, Sherry Smith met up with another
young lefty with the moniker of George Herman Ruth,
nicknamed "The Babe." The game was labeled a "double
masterpiece" and a 'hitters' nightmare." Through thirteen
innings, both Smith and Ruth had allowed only six hits and one

run, and Ruth gave up an inside-the-park home run to Henry "Hy" Myers in the first inning. In the third, Ruth knocked in the tying run with a ground out. In the bottom of the fourteenth, Dick Hoblitzell started a dramatic finish by drawing his fourth walk of the game. Duffy Lewis followed this by sacrificing Hoblitzell into scoring position at second base. Red Sox manager Bill Carrigan made the correct decision by sending in Mike McNally as a pinch-runner and putting Del Gainor in as a pinch-hitter. Gainor stepped up to the plate driving in Hoblitzell and sealed Boston's 2-1 victory. Just as in game one, nobody dominated. One team just outlasted the other. It could have gone either way but didn't. This game has always been one of the most classic games in World Series History.

In game three at Brooklyn, manager Wilbert Robinson turned to another Series veteran, right-hander Jack Coombs. It was the first World Series game ever to be played at the recently erected Ebbets Field. (1913) Coombs needed relief from Jeff Pfeffer to pitch a 4-3 victory that put his team back into World Series contention. Again, it can hardly be said that one team dominated the other. The Robins simply outlasted the Red Sox.

Game four was at Ebbets Field. In the first inning, Brooklyn's first three batters reached safely. Dutch Leonard wound up giving up two runs. Leonard shut the door, and that's all the Dodgers would get. Larry Gardner's second home run in two days in the second inning was an inside-the-parker to left-center that scored two teammates ahead of him, giving Leonard all he'd need to win.

In game five, played at Braves Field, it took only one hour and forty-three minutes to complete the festivities. Game one winner Ernie Shore threw a three-hitter. Boston scratched out a run on a walk, sacrifice bunt, groundout, and passed ball. Thanks to an error, the Red Sox added two in the third and a Chick Shorten RBI single. In the fifth, Harry Hooper singled and scored on a Hal Janvrin double. Casey Stengel led off the Dodger ninth with a hit, but Shore allowed nothing else. For the second series in a row, Red Sox pitching dominated, this time holding the Robins to a team .200 batting average which strongly contributed to their series victory.

As with all such competitions, there were some memorable moments. Ernie Shaw won two games. Casey Stengel went 4 for 11, hitting .364. There were two saves recorded for the first time in World Series History. (Carl Mays and Jeff Pfeffer) Dutch Leonard and Babe Ruth had dominating pitching performances. The Series featured 3 home runs, but only one was hit out of the park. Future Hall of Famer Rube Marquard lost 2 games. Boston only used five pitchers in the entire Series.

Winning manager Bill Carrigan retired and went into banking in Maine after the 1916 World Series. He was only the manager for four years, winning two World Series in 1915 and 1916. He tried to return as a manager in the twenties, but his teams all finished in last place.

Although the loss of the World Series was disappointing, 1916 was one of the most successful seasons in the History of the team. 447,747 fans thronged to the park doubling the prior year's attendance. The long-suffering fans finally had a winner, and Ebbets' finances were on the black side. Ebbets was exhausted, and there were rumors of him selling the team. His assessment was, "I need a rest badly."

With the threatening gray skies of winter about to envelop the Northeast, these same clouds splashed tears of loss to a mighty team that had gone down in defeat. When the final petal of Fall was finally picked, Charles H. Ebbets had to face yet another winter of musings. Undoubtedly, he returned to his office at Ebbets Field to face another winter of storms. He would have one last chance to make it real.

1916 National League Champion Brooklyn "Robins'
Wilbert Robinson above Batboy

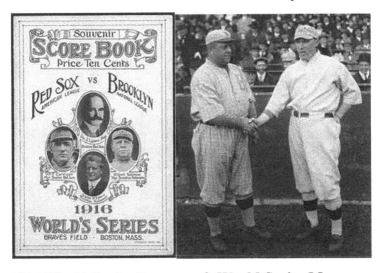

1916 World Series Program & World Series Managers
Wilbert Robinson & Bill Carrigan

191

Summary

AL Boston Red Sox (4) vs. NL Brooklyn Robins (1)

Game	Date	Score	Location	Time	Attendance
1	October 7	Brooklyn Robins – 5, **Boston Red Sox** – 6	Braves Field	2:16	36,117
2	October 9	Brooklyn Robins – 1, **Boston Red Sox** – 2 (14 innings)	Braves Field	2:32	47,373
3	October 10	Boston Red Sox – 3, **Brooklyn Robins** – 4	Ebbets Field	2:01	21,087
4	October 11	**Boston Red Sox** – 6, Brooklyn Robins – 2	Ebbets Field	2:30	21,662
5	October 12	Brooklyn Robins – 1, **Boston Red Sox** – 4	Braves Field	1:43	43,620

Game 1

Saturday, October 7, 1916, 2:00 PM (ET) at Braves Field in Boston, Massachusetts

Team	1	2	3	4	5	6	7	8	9	R	H	E
Brooklyn	0	0	0	1	0	0	0	0	4	5	10	4
Boston	0	0	1	0	1	0	3	1	X	6	8	1

192

WP: Ernie Shore (1–0)   **LP:** Rube Marquard (0–1)   **Save:** Carl Mays (1)

Ernie Shaw   **Rube Marquard**   **Carl Mays**   **Fred Merkle**

Game 2

Monday, October 9, 1916, 2:00 PM (ET) at Braves Field in Boston, Massachusetts

Team	1	2	3	4	5	6	7	8	9	10	11	12	13	14	R	H	E
Brooklyn	1	0	0	0	0	0	0	0	0	0	0	0	0	0	1	6	2
Boston	0	0	1	0	0	0	0	0	0	0	0	0	0	1	2	7	1

WP: Babe Ruth (1–0)   **LP:** Sherrod (Sherry) Smith (0–1)

Home runs: BKN: Hy Myers (1) BOS: None

Babe Ruth   Sherry Smith   Henry "Hy" Myers   Del Gainer

Game 3

Tuesday, October 10, 1916, 2:00 PM (ET) at Ebbets Field in Brooklyn, New York

Team	1	2	3	4	5	6	7	8	9	R	H	E
Boston	0	0	0	0	0	2	1	0	0	3	7	1
Brooklyn	0	0	1	1	2	0	0	0	X	4	10	0

WP: Jack Coombs (1–0) **LP:** Carl Mays (0–1) **Sv:** Jeff Pfeffer (1)

Home runs: BOS: Larry Gardner (1) Bkln: None

Jack Coombs, Carl Mays, Jeff Pfeffer, Larry Gardiner

Game 4

Wednesday, October 11, 1916, 2:00 PM (ET) at Ebbets Field in Brooklyn, New York

Team	1	2	3	4	5	6	7	8	9	R	H	E
Boston	0	3	0	1	1	0	1	0	0	6	10	1
Brooklyn	2	0	0	0	0	0	0	0	0	2	5	4

WP: Dutch Leonard (1–0) **LP:** Rube Marquard (0–2)

Home runs: BOS: Larry Gardner (2) BKN: None

Dutch Leonard   Rube Marquard   Larry Gardiner

Game 5

Thursday, October 12, 1916, 2:00 PM (ET) at Braves Field in Boston, Massachusetts

Team	1	2	3	4	5	6	7	8	9	R	H	E
Brooklyn	0	1	0	0	0	0	0	0	0	**1**	**3**	**3**
Boston	0	1	2	0	1	0	0	0	X	**4**	**7**	**2**

WP: Ernie Shore (2–0)   **LP:** Jeff Pfeffer (0–1)

Ernie Shore Chick Shorten Harry Hooper Hal Janvrin Casey Stengel

CHAPTER TWENTY-FIVE
Into the Void

1916 would be a hard season to replicate. That team was built to win for just one season based on aging pitching. In some fashion, baseball reflects what is going on historically. It was graphically demonstrated by *Ken Burns' Baseball* series. 1917 would be no different. Player salaries before the Federal League war were held at the $2400 level for the most part. After that time, salaries skyrocketed. Charles Ebbets knew two things. The 1916 players would want a reward for their championship season. He also knew that the team would be in dire financial straits without a repeat. World War 1 was looming, so the next three years were likely to be a challenge regardless of what he did. 25-cent seats were still an issue. By adding aisles in some of the bleacher areas, he raised those prices. Ebbets, quite the roque, persuaded the local building inspector to order him to do so!

Ebbets argued to the other magnates that cheap seats and high salaries caused by the inflated federal league prices for players spelled doom. Charlie claimed that 1916 salaries and bonuses cost him $125,000. (Just under $2 million today).

Baseball today has many sources of income that didn't exist in 1916. For the most part, current-day owners are tied to powerful money-making machines. In Brooklyn, it was just

Charlie, Ed, and Steve. The Yankees and Cardinals would often win if we peer slightly into the future. The Yankees were funded by Jake Rupert's beer money. August Busch's beer money funded the Cardinals. Everywhere else, income was based on ticket sales. The formula was simple no ticket sales equals no team. From the fan perspective, it was equally simple. No team equals no ticket purchases.

Given this, Ebbets sought to cut player salaries. It would not be taken well by the players. Ebbets was labeled as both cheap and ungrateful. What they said about him behind his back could not be printed. Tom Rice of the *"Brooklyn Eagle"* said that Ebbets was a frequent target of ridicule, "much of which is vicious," and that "he was abused in language both libelous and inexcusable." All the newsprint about him over his time with the Brooklyn team must have also taken its toll. He did the best with what he had and exhibited all the human flaws that anyone who walked this earth might have.

His first two targets were Casey Stengel and Zach Wheat. Stengel had used the Federal League war to negotiate his salary from the $3,000 level up to the $5,300 level. Stengel, his entire life, was known to be irascible. Casey would yield to no one. His favorite targets were umpires. Casey argued, and Ebbets labeled him as impudent. Stengel went public by complaining to the *"Brooklyn Eagle."* He also had just hit .364 in the 1916 World Series. Casey thought he deserved a "nice little increase" Ebbets argued that Casey had been ill in 1915 and that he was still paid his salary.

Regardless Casey went into the Spring of 1917 unsigned. It went on tit for tat with no resolution and was visibly seen in the press. Stengel's salary was the equivalent of Zach Wheat's. In the long run, Casey settled for $3,600 with a possible bonus of $400 if he hit .300. He hit .257 and led the team with 6 home runs and 73 runs batted in for the 1917 season. Such a bitter battle was not likely to end here. Casey was traded to the Pittsburgh Pirates along with second baseman George Cutshaw for future hall of fame pitcher Burleigh Grimes, pitcher Al Mamaux and infielder Chuck Ward in 1918.

Charlie Ebbets also wanted Zach Wheat to take a pay cut. The future Hall of Fame outfielder was miffed by the offer. In both cases, Ebbets tried to act that any salary increase caused by the Federal League war should be rolled back because that league lost the war. Players would never agree. Unlike Stengel, Wheat did not argue through the press. Ebbets heard nothing from Wheat, so he went to press instead, arguing that Wheat was given two straight salary increases but now wanted a third. The supposed increase was to be a 20% increase. Ebbets also intimated that he was open to compromise. A deal was hammered out where Wheat kept his $5,300 salary with the potential for a bonus if he hit over .300 again. This potential reached Wheat, and he decided to show up for spring training unsigned. Wheat hit .312 in 1917 and received his bonus. Wheat was probably the best offensive player Brooklyn had in its first 50 years. The era he hit in was called the dead-ball era. Zach Wheat ended his career in 1927 with a career batting average of .317 and 132 home runs over 19 years. The long ball era began in 1920 when Babe Ruth went from 29 to 54 home runs in 1919.

Another potential nightmare for Ebbets and baseball happened in 1917 when the United States entered World War 1. Ebbets' fears soon became a reality. A 10% war tax was levied on ticket sales. The magnates already paid Corporate and Income Taxes. Major League Baseball had no choice but to pass the increase to the fans. Those same fans now had their attention taken from the Sports Page to the Main Page. Many players went away to fight in the "Great War," as it was called then.

The owners met and decided to end the regular 1918 season. On September 1, 1918, the Federal government ordered A "Work or Fight" edict. The World Series was held early (September 5th -11th), with the Red Sox defeating the Cubs. By mid-September, Ebbets Field was being used to hold military war supplies.

Ebbets decided to stop paying the players whose salaries weren't being supported with game income. First Baseman Jake Daubert was not paid the remainder of his annual salary, which left him short $2150. Daubert appealed to the National Commission, which was a magnate-based committee. They naturally sided with Ebbets. Daubert, not dissuaded, found lawyer John Montgomery Ward to represent him. Lawyer Ward was formerly the Brooklyn team manager at Eastern Park. It was not good news for Ebbets. Charlie got so upset that he swore that Daubert would never play another game for Brooklyn. He then traded Daubert to Cincinnati for Tommy Griffin, who was nowhere near an equivalent player. The lawsuit was eventually settled for $1500 to be paid in $500 increments. Ebbets was not gracious in losing and spitefully delayed payments to Daubert.

World War 1 ended on November 11, 1918. An estimated 126,000 U.S. soldiers were killed out of nearly 10 million deaths. Fans returned in droves in 1919, wanting to celebrate merriment over bereavement. Returning from the war were Brooklyn pitchers Leon Cadore, Jeff Pfeffer, and Sherry Smith giving Brooklyn its pitching depth back.

During the war, Charlie Ebbets tried a ploy that totally backfired but eventually bore fruit. He scheduled a Sunday Game with the Phillies at Ebbets Field for July 1, 1917. It was masked by a Sunday concert of patriotic and religious music. The game would follow the concert. Admission was supposedly only charged for the concert. The proceeds were to be donated to various war relief organizations. The local authorities were not impressed by this generous offer. They confirmed that admission was being charged for the baseball game and arrested Ebbets and the two McKeevers for violating Sunday Blue Laws. All three were convicted.

These arrests led to favorable press coverage that eventually helped sway sentiment. Some argued that the Sabbath was kept holy by attending Sunday Morning services and that, having completed their obligation, they were free to do whatever they wanted in the afternoon. By 1918 the movie and media industry, along with the three New York Baseball clubs, found allies among progressive and labor contingencies. Manhattan State Senator Jimmy Walker proposed a bill to repeal the Sunday Blue Laws ban on entertainment. Businesses would have to wait to have their shackles removed on Sundays until 1963 in New York. The bill was passed in both state legislatures on April 19, 1919 and approved (64-0) by the New York City Board of Alderman some ten days later.

Charles Ebbets wasted no time scheduling a Sunday game and saw 22,000 fans attend without advanced sales. The magnates called a special meeting to rearrange the rest of the 1919 season. Brooklyn was given 13 Sunday dates, while at the Polo Grounds, the Giants were given 10. They also shared the Polo Grounds with the Yankees, who would move to a newly built Yankee Stadium in 1922.

In the long run, the war was ending, and the blue law repeal probably saved Charles Ebbets bacon. He did not realize it, but with the clock ticking, he only had one more chance left, and that chance was about to knock on his door.

CHAPTER TWENTY-SIX
The 1920 World Series

Charles Ebbets finally got his wish at the February 1920 owner's meeting. The 25-cent ticket was finally eliminated. The price structure went from 25/50/75 to 50/75/1.00. In addition, Brooklyn had 19 new Sabbath day games scheduled at Ebbets Field. Club finances would finally be bolstered.

On the field, the team still had a shaky shortstop and a porous infield defense. The situation wasn't solved until Pee Wee Reese showed up some twenty years later. Opening day saw the team defeat the Philadelphia Phillies 9-2 behind the pitching of Leon Cadore. 10,000 fans showed up. An estimated 56,000 fans attended the first two Sunday games. It demonstrates the importance of Sunday games.

Early in the season, an event stood out in baseball's annals. The event occurred on May 1, 1920. It was a pitching duel between Leon Cadore of Brooklyn and Joe Oeschger (pronounced Eshker) of the Braves.

The game started at 3 PM at Braves Field in Boston and lasted until 6:50, when umpire Bill McCormick called it, despite appeals from the players to go one more inning so they could say they played three complete games. It was also the first day of daylight savings, so if the game had been played a day earlier, it would have been called well before the 26th inning

1919 W514 Dodger Cards from authors Dodger Museum collection

The New York Times reported that "Joe Oeschger and Leon Cadore were the real outstanding heroes among a score of heroes in the monumental affray of this afternoon. ... Instead of showing any signs of weakening under strain, each of them appeared to grow stronger. In the final six innings, neither artist allowed even the shadow of a safe single." The closest a team came to a win happened in the 17th inning when Brooklyn loaded the bases with one out. The next batter grounded back to Oeschger, who got the force out at home. Still, the throw to first to complete the double play was in the dirt, and Ed Konetchy tried to score from third, only to get thrown out at home with Boston catcher Hank Gowdy making a diving tag on Konetchy's spikes. Leon Cadore faced 96 batters and Joe Oeschger 90. Conservatively estimating an average of three pitches per batter, each pitcher threw nearly 300 pitches. Consider today when at 100 pitches, a pitcher is done.

Neither pitcher threw again for more than a week. Leon Cadore said he couldn't raise his arm for three days to comb his hair but returned and had a good season, helping Brooklyn reach the World Series.

Leon Cadore married Charles Ebbets' daughter Lydie Mae in 1931. After his baseball career, he worked on Wall Street until the stock market crash in 1929. He then moved to Idaho to mine copper.

Leon Cadore   Joe Oeschger

Brooklyn won 23 of its last 29 games finishing 7 games ahead of the New York Giants.

204

In 1919 the magnates decided to make the World Series a best of nine games. The apparent reason was to make more money. This same format was followed in 1920. The first three games were scheduled for Ebbets Field. Nine Brooklyn players were returning from the 1916 Series. They were pitchers Marquard, Pfeffer, Smith, and Wheat, Miller, Myers, Johnson, and Olson.

A major controversy arose in the 1919 World Series about a gambling fix. Eight members of the Chicago White Sox were all charged with conspiring to throw the Fall Classic against the Cincinnati Reds. After a lengthy investigation and a highly publicized trial in 1921, the Black Sox were acquitted despite their confessions. They later disputed the story. All the players involved were subsequently banned from baseball because of their undeniable link to gamblers and Arnold Rothstein. This event caused baseball to appoint Judge Kenesaw Mountain Landis as the commissioner of Baseball. It was good news for baseball but bad news for African American players integrating baseball, according to some. Others blamed the owners. Throughout the 1920 season, league offices constantly denied accusations from the press that professional baseball was in on the take and made every effort to assuage the fans that the 1919 scandal was an isolated incident. To win back fans' approval, the commissioner went to great lengths to promote the integrity of baseball in the papers. Still, many wondered if the fan's trust in baseball and the World Series would fully recover. Only time would tell as the Brooklyn team returned for their second series appearance. This time it was against the Cleveland Indians. The first three games took place at Ebbets Field.

Unfortunately, that exploit was not on the field. In Game 1, Cleveland's starting pitcher Stan Coveleski silenced Brooklyn's line-up in a five-hit, 3-1 opening game win. Ed Konechty drove in Zach Wheat in the fifth inning, who doubled for Brooklyn's only tally. Rube Marquard had lost his third straight World Series game for Brooklyn dating back to 1916. Rube would see more action later in the series.

In game 2, Burleigh Grimes tossed a seven-hit shutout that ended in a 3-0 series-tying victory. Zach Wheat drove in one run, Tommy Griffith two.

In game 3, Sherry Smith threw a 2-1 three-hitter with Zach Wheat and Hy Myers driving in the two Brooklyn runs. The Series then switched to Cleveland's Dunn Field, with Brooklyn ahead two games to one.

 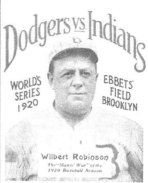

1920 World Series Managers Tris Speaker & Wilbert Robinson World Series Program.

Extra left-field seats were added to Ebbets Field for the 1920 World Series

Controversy arose when pitcher Rube Marquard was arrested for ticket scalping before game four. According to Marquard's biographer Larry Mansch, Marquard was in the lobby of the Winton Hotel in Cleveland when he offered an acquaintance from Brooklyn tickets at above the stated ticket price. Regrettably, the conversation was overheard by a detective who arrested Marquard and brought him to the Cleveland jail. He was released on his own recognizance but had to return the next day for a trial. He was found guilty and paid a $1 fine with $3.80 in court costs. Given the Black Sox scandal the year prior, Marquard did not know the firestorm he had just unleashed. 400 sports scribes looking for grist for their mills now had a story to tell between the series switch from Brooklyn to Cleveland. The illuminators unleashed the full wrath of Noah Webster against Marquard. Marquard paid it no regard, which was a mistake. The feathers of Ebbets and the McKeevers, along with league president Heydler, were indubitably ruffled. Ebbets had recently chided ticket scalpers outside Ebbets Field about plying their trade, so he was not going to take this from one of his employees. Ebbets was through with Marquard and traded him to Cincinnati that winter. Rube still had three good years left in his hall of fame career, winning 17 for Cincinnati in 1921.

Hot Dogs and Ticket Sales at Ebbets Field in 1920

In game 4, Stan Coveleski returned to defeat Brooklyn 5-1. Leon Cadore, of 26-inning game fame, was knocked out in the first inning. Brooklyn never came back. Tommy Griffith knocked in Brooklyn's lone run.

With the Series tied at two games apiece, Brooklyn's Burleigh Grimes had a second go at Cleveland's pitcher Jim Bagby. The Indian's line-up came out swinging and immediately loaded the bases in the bottom of the first. Elmer Smith stepped up to the plate and into the record books by smashing the first grand slam home run in World Series history. The historic blast sent the home team crowd into an earsplitting frenzy that set the tenor for the rest of the game. The score remained 4-0 until the fourth when pitcher Bagby hit a three-run homer. With a 7-0 lead, the Indians had a lock on the game. Brooklyn had not scored but was headed on the right track with Pete Kilduff and Otto Miller on base and in scoring position. Clarence Mitchell, who had come in the game in the fourth, was Brooklyn's next hitter. Mitchell, who was generally used as a pinch-hitter, outfielder, and utility infielder, hit a sharp line drive to second baseman Bill Wambsganss who caught the ball, stepped on the bag, and tagged out a returning Miller to complete the first unassisted triple play in World Series history. After scoring a run in the ninth, Brooklyn fell to the Indians in an 8-1 loss.

The Wambsganss Triple Play

In game 6, Walter Mails, recently acquired from Brooklyn, threw a superb three-hit, 1-0 shutout to defeat his former teammates.

In game 7, future hall of fame pitcher Stan Coveleski returned for his third five-hitter of the Series in a 3-0 masterwork. Remarkably, the Indian's pitching staff had held Brooklyn to just two runs in the final forty-three innings of the Series on their way to their first World Championship.

Burleigh Grimes   Stan Coveleski

Bill Wambsganss   Ray Chapman

The victory was bittersweet as the team was still convalescing from losing one of its players. Shortstop Ray Chapman known for excellent defense and leadership died after being struck in the head by a pitch by Carl Mays of the Yankees while playing in New York. His teammates had endured and won the World Series. They dedicated their win to his memory.

Charles Ebbets faced yet another winter of doubts but had things to be happy about. Finances, always a problem, saw a dramatic turnaround. Ebbets Field saw a record-breaking 800,000 fans come through the turnstiles. They also got to share in the gate receipts of seven World Series games. Ebbets would come close one more time in 1924 thanks to the pitching combination of Hall of Fame pitchers Dazzy Vance and Burleigh Grimes but would never see his charges make it back to the World Series.

AL <u>Cleveland Indians</u> (5) vs. NL <u>Brooklyn Robins</u> (2)

Game	Date	Score	Location	Time	Attendance
1	October 5	**Cleveland Indians –** 3, Brooklyn Robins – 1	Ebbets Field	1:41	23,573
2	October 6	Cleveland Indians – 0, **Brooklyn Robins – 3**	Ebbets Field	1:55	22,559
3	October 7	Cleveland Indians – 1, **Brooklyn Robins – 2**	Ebbets Field	1:47	25,088
4	October 9	Brooklyn Robins – 1, **Cleveland Indians – 5**	League Park	1:54	25,734
5	October 10	Brooklyn Robins – 1, **Cleveland Indians – 8**	League Park	1:49	26,884
6	October 11	Brooklyn Robins – 0, **Cleveland Indians – 1**	League Park	1:34	27,194
7	October 12	Brooklyn Robins – 0, **Cleveland Indians – 3**	League Park	1:55	27,525

Game 1

Tuesday, October 5, 1920, 2:00 PM (<u>ET</u>) at <u>Ebbets Field</u> in <u>Brooklyn</u>, <u>New York</u>

211

Team	1	2	3	4	5	6	7	8	9	R	H	E
Cleveland	0	2	0	1	0	0	0	0	0	3	5	0
Brooklyn	0	0	0	0	0	0	1	0	0	1	5	1

WP: Stan Coveleski (1–0)   **LP:** Rube Marquard (0–1)

Stan Coveleski   Ed Konechty   Zach Wheat   Rube Marquard

Game 2

Wednesday, October 6, 1920, 2:00 PM (ET) at Ebbets Field in Brooklyn, New York

Team	1	2	3	4	5	6	7	8	9	R	H	E
Cleveland	0	0	0	0	0	0	0	0	0	0	7	1
Brooklyn	1	0	1	0	1	0	0	0	X	3	7	0

WP: Burleigh Grimes (1–0)   **LP:** Jim Bagby (0–1)

Burleigh Grimes   Zach Wheat   Tommy Griffith

Game 3

Thursday, October 7, 1920, 2:00 PM (ET) at Ebbets Field in Brooklyn, New York

Team	1	2	3	4	5	6	7	8	9	**R**	**H**	**E**
Cleveland	0	0	0	1	0	0	0	0	0	1	3	1
Brooklyn	2	0	0	0	0	0	0	0	X	**2**	**6**	**1**

WP: Sherry Smith (1–0) **LP:** Ray Caldwell (0–1)

Sherry Smith   **Zach Wheat**   **Henry "Hy" Myers**

Game 4

Saturday, October 9, 1920, 2:00 PM (ET) at League Park in Cleveland, Ohio

Team	1	2	3	4	5	6	7	8	9	**R**	**H**	**E**
Brooklyn	0	0	0	1	0	0	0	0	0	**1**	**5**	**1**
Cleveland	2	0	2	0	0	1	0	0	X	**5**	**12**	**2**

WP: Stan Coveleski (2–0) **LP:** Leon Cadore (0–1)

Stan Coveleski, Leon Cadore, Tommy Griffith

Game 5

Sunday, October 10, 1920, 2:00 PM (ET) at League Park in Cleveland, Ohio

Team	1	2	3	4	5	6	7	8	9	R	H	E
Brooklyn	0	0	0	0	0	0	0	0	1	1	13	1
Cleveland	4	0	0	3	1	0	0	0	X	**8**	12	2

WP: Jim Bagby (1–1) **LP:** Burleigh Grimes (1–1)

Home runs: BRO: None CLE: Elmer Smith (1), Jim Bagby (1)

Jim Bagby   **Burleigh Grimes**   **Elmer Smith**

Otto Miller   **Pete Kilduff**   **Bill Wambsganss**

214

Game 6

Monday, October 11, 1920, 2:00 PM (ET) at League Park in Cleveland, Ohio

Team	1	2	3	4	5	6	7	8	9	R	H	E
Brooklyn	0	0	0	0	0	0	0	0	0	0	3	0
Cleveland	0	0	0	0	0	1	0	0	X	1	7	3

WP: Duster Mails (1–0) **LP:** Sherry Smith (1–1)

Duster Mails   George Burns   Tris Speaker

Game 7

Tuesday, October 12, 1920, 2:00 PM (ET) at League Park in Cleveland, Ohio

Team	1	2	3	4	5	6	7	8	9	R	H	E
Brooklyn	0	0	0	0	0	0	0	0	0	0	5	2
Cleveland	0	0	0	1	1	0	1	0	X	3	7	3

WP: Stan Coveleski (3–0) **LP:** Burleigh Grimes (1–2)

Stan Coveleski   **Burleigh Grimes**   **Tris Speaker**

CHAPTER TWENTY-SEVEN
The End of Spring

On October 29, 1920, shortly after the 1920 World Series, Charles Ebbets turned 61. As 1921 commenced, bronchitis confined Charlie to his house for over three weeks. Illness and contentious contract negotiations would now dominate the rest of his life. He probably should have sold his interest in the team and left. A nervous system only has so many miles on it, so to speak. He was addicted to the adrenalin rush caused by his notoriety. He also was outrageously stubborn, exhibiting temper tantrums.

Pat Moran, Wilbert Robinson & a visibly heavier Charles Ebbets on the right in 1921.

After the December 1922 owner's meeting, Ebbets took an extensive tour of Europe with his second wife, Grace. It was reported that he was powerless "to walk twenty-five yards without breathing heavily." After returning from Europe, he divulged that he would build a cottage near the team's spring training facilities in Clearwater, Florida. He became a winter resident because the warmer climate improved his bronchitis and neuritis. Ebbets had been having problems with the cold winters of New York for several years prior. In August 1923, Charlie took an in-season vacation back to Clearwater, Florida. His bronchial problems returned as soon as he returned to the cold of the north. Given his health issues, he probably should have been thinking about the club in the event of his death. Not doing so, along with other factors, would throw the team into turmoil for over a dozen years after his death.

At least he did not have to worry about club finances any longer. There was now a broader interest in baseball, and Sunday games made teams more profitable. As he headed south for the winter in 1923, he told the media that the 1924 contracts had not been signed because he had been "too ill to think of the business." Ebbets had lost 30 pounds and claimed to be getting better. Herbert Casey, his doctor, claimed his blood pressure was normal for a 64-year-old man. The doctor warned him not to get all riled up as his heart was not in the greatest of conditions to handle it.

The last thing Charlie needed was contentious salary arbitrations. That was precisely what he got. The petitioners this time were future hall of fame pitchers Burleigh Grimes and Dazzy Vance. After sparring with both for several rounds of negotiations, the *Brooklyn Eagle* finally reported that "the Squire's coat is off, and he is in the ring fighting," something a man with a heart condition should not be doing. It is doubtful that he could have turned these negotiations over to the McKeevers as that was not their bailiwick. Besides, Ebbets was just too stubborn and not of an even temperament.

Hall of Famers "Spitballer" Burleigh Grimes and Dazzy Vance

Ebbets then hosted a visit by Judge Kenesaw Mountain Landis, which his doctor advised him not to do. The next day, Ebbets went to the park but could not leave his car, which was blamed on his neuritis (nerve inflammation).

Prophetically, the *Brooklyn Eagle* noted, "Trouble with leading players has been a handicap to his return to health." A few days later, Ebbets was described as "seriously ill" and "confined to his bed." Although his condition was reported to be improving, the situation rapidly deteriorated. There was a portentous report on April 17 that he had "taken a turn for the worse." That turn could not be reversed, and on April 18, 1925, at 6:05 PM, Ebbets died. His funeral was held at the Holy Trinity Church in Brooklyn, and he was interred at Greenwood Cemetery, not far from his friend Henry Chadwick "the Father of Baseball." Ebbets Attorney Bernard J. York had died the week prior, and at Ebbets funeral, co-owner Ed McKeever caught pneumonia and died the following week. The three friends that ran the team were all gone in less than a month, leaving Steve McKeever to run the show. Ed McKeever had no children, so Steve had control of Ed's 25% of the club and his own 25%. The Ebbets family controlled the other 50%, divided 15 ways. It was a certainty that nothing would ever be agreed to. It was a looming storm of unimagined proportions. With the death of Charles Ebbets, all the Boys of Spring were gone: Charles Byrne in 1898; Joseph J. Doyle in 1908; George J. Taylor in 1911; and Gus Abell in 1913. Ebbets was the last in 1925. With all their faults and foibles, these were the men who started it all.

Epilogue

Charles Ebbets had given significant thought to the division of his accrued wealth among two wives and four children who were at odds over the bitterness surrounding Charles' divorce. In his youth, Ebbets was forced to marry his first wife, Minnie, because he got her pregnant. The resultant child was Charles Ebbets Jr. Apparently, this rubbed Charlie the wrong way because he would not have chosen Minnie but did "the right thing" at the time. As he got older, he regretted the decision and wanted to make his own choice. He found the divorcee' Grace Slade Nott and wanted her as a replacement for Minnie. It was not a world of simple divorces, and the details found their way into the press. Steve McKeever read all the details and found a religious basis for his hate of Charlie. "Thou shalt not covet thy neighbor's wife" was etched in stone for him. Steve wanted no dealings with a family with a divorce in it. Charlies' daughter Lydie Mae divorced her husband Frank Hendricks, who worked in Real Estate sales in Manhattan, in 1914. Then she got married again in 1931 to former Dodger pitcher Leon Cadore. With Charles Ebbet's divorce, Steve McKeever was seething in hate because he saw the work of the devil operative here. Ed McKeever, the brain and boss of the McKeever clan, told his older brother it was none of his business. He further stated that whatever went on in other people's private lives was only their personal concern. Their relationship was purely business in nature. Ed told Steve to keep his grumbling to himself. Steve was unmoved but was checkmated by Ed and attorney Bernard J. York while they still lived.

Steve's next target was Wilbert Robinson, who he felt was the devil's consort. At one point, he threw an ink well at "Uncle Robbie," forcing him to move his office to a little room in the clubhouse near the right-field stands. Steve McKeever became the acting team president until Wilbert Robinson was elected team president on May 25, 1925. It further enraged McKeever. With Ebbets, Bernie, and Ed dead, Steve wreaked havoc on all the sinners to punish them in the name of God. It got to the point where the Ebbets and McKeevers would sit in different parts of the park to avoid having contact with each other. At the park, the Ebbets ladies sat behind the 1st base dugout, and the McKeever ladies sat behind the 3rd base one.

Charles Jr. was thrown out of the park twice and was allegedly assaulted by Steve McKeever. Charlie Jr. sued McKeever for $20,000, and after various ploys and counter ploys, the case was finally settled out of court. Let's not forget that Charlie Jr. was still the club Secretary and part-owner. The younger Ebbets, not to be left out of the fray, had been sent to Bill Brown's Physical Cultural Farm that was established for "building up broken down businessmen." The Dodger family was loaded with dysfunction. It would not go away. The Three Stooges would have a hard time topping this dramatic comedy act. It played far better than the team on the ball grounds. The game on the playing field was kept on automatic pilot until 1937. The internecine warfare between the families dominated everything else. In that period, 6th place was the usual position the team landed. There was a fluke year where the Dodgers made it to third place. There was no captain of the ship, only inmates! Steve McKeevers's hate made $1,766,972 worth of Dodger

222

stock profitless for 16 years from 1925 to 1941. Hate and religious beliefs were worth more than money. Baseball and winning were nowhere on this table.

What Monseigneur Ludeke, Steve McKeever's "great friend," role was in loading this cannon can only be imagined. No doubt, his religious indoctrination helped temper Steve's judgment. Many such "preachers" were of the fire and brimstone variety. The words in the Bible, even though contradictory at times, were thought to be some direct conduit from God. Armageddon, retribution and an account reckoning one's life were primal in this view. The "Judge" must have thought he was on the committee to decide. It didn't occur to McKeever that hate was not a "godly" virtue. Nowhere in his credo was forgiveness and making amends.

Steve McKeever drank milk daily. He sat in the last row of seats at Ebbets Field with his good friend Roman Catholic Monseigneur F. X. Ludeke and had a drink of milk in the third inning. On the other side of the spectrum, his doctors told Uncle Robbie to limit his whisky drinking to three a day. Uncle Robbie took that to mean three full tumblers.

Wilbert Robinson told a New York Managing editor that his sportswriter was getting a $1000 Christmas gift from the club every year. It added fuel to the hate fire. From then on, Steve McKeever referred to Uncle Robbie as "the Squealer." In 1929 the National League stepped in "to bring some order out of the chaos by appointing Frank York friendly to both sides as president of the club." (According to the New York's *Daily News* of September 28, 1941) Frank was attorney Bernard J. York's son. McKeever was checkmated for several years but finally got rid of the "rat" Robinson at the end of the 1931 seasons.

In any event, Robinson was only a shell of his former self. He managed from 1914 until 1931, until Steve McKeever indirectly deposed him. Throughout this time, the team was called "the Robins" in deference to their portly manager. "Uncle Robbie" was given the news while fishing for shad near Butler Island, Georgia. He dropped his net and went to a nearby bar where he supposedly stayed for a week. Wilbert Robinson died a broken man less than three years later. To complete the coup Max Carey was appointed manager of the team, and the name "Dodgers" was immediately splashed across the team's jersey, which remains until today. It was the last nail in the coffin of Robinson and his "Robins." Steve McKeever wanted no vestiges of "Uncle Robbie" left. The name "Robins" was an abomination to him. Hence "Dodgers" became the team's official name from that point forward because of hate.

Ebbets' will was filed in probate court on May 6, 1925. It provided housing for both Grace and Minnie. It also confirmed Minnie's alimony settlement and gave Charles Jr. a $2000 annual annuity. He also left a $5000 fund for his friends to celebrate his birthday yearly. Ebbets knew that his various family members were divided due to Minnie's divorce. He then stipulated that anyone who challenged his will would be eliminated from receiving any of it. All his shares in the team were divided amongst his 15 heirs into equal parts. On the other hand, Steve signed over his 25 percent share in the club to his daughter "Dearie," who married James Mulvey. He maintained his brother's 25% ownership shares as Ed had no children as heirs.

In the meantime, the Mechanics Bank merged with the Brooklyn Trust Co. in 1929. George McLaughlin, head of the Bank, viewed the Bank's loans to their heirs against their dividends. The debt was mounting. He cut out payments. The Ebbets family, few of whom had worked, shrieked. Lydie Mae blamed the change on Robinson's dismissal.

The Bank appointed Larry MacPhail to run the club. MacPhail, Joseph Gilleaudeau, Ebbets executor and son-in-law, stayed on the club's board of directors. The Ebbets family asked for an accounting. The case dragged on for four years.

His One True Love

For every ton of hate Steve McKeever had for the Ebbets family and for Uncle Robbie, he had a double amount of love for his daughter, Dearie, with whom he is shown. Sixteen years ago he gave Dearie, now Mrs. James Mulvey, his 25% interest in the Dodgers.

In any event, the consequence of the fight was a decision made by Surrogate Judge Wingate. He said the executors were to be applauded for their efforts. But by this time, Banker George McLaughlin knew that he'd have to get into the baseball business whether he wanted to or not. Even though the Dodgers fans were more enthusiastic than ever and over 300,000 showed up yearly, the Dodgers fell on hard times. The depression could be blamed for some of it. By the end of 1937, phone service had been cut off at Ebbets Field because the bills weren't being paid. It wasn't uncommon for process servers to be seen seeking payment for unpaid bills. After years of neglect, Ebbets Field was an assemblage of broken seats with poor bathrooms and broken-down plumbing. Even the beautiful rotunda was covered in mildew. Maintenance was not in this group's vocabulary. Debt was piling on debt in the Dodgers account. With the agreement from the McKeever interests, George McLaughlin of the Brooklyn Trust Co. decided that the only way to wipe out the debt was to open his checkbook. He hired a manager who knew his business and gave him carte blanche to build a winning team. He appointed Larry MacPhail, whose first official duty, ironically enough, was to attend the funeral of the "Master of Hate," Steve McKeever. Steve's death on March 7, 1938, was a blessing in disguise. First, he would have fought against losing his cherished power. In the second, confusion, disorganization, and intrigue immediately gave way to peace and harmony. Steve's nickname "The Judge" was oddly appropriate as all he ever did was judge everyone and everything based on his myopic vision. With Steve's passing, the club was in peculiar hands. True, Dearie's husband, James Mulvey, was still on the board, as was Joseph Gilleaudeau, Genevieve Ebbets's husband who left after 1944, as did Grace Slade Ebbets, Charlie's second wife.

All the others were out. Dearie's heirs would later sell their interest to Walter O'Malley in 1975, ending all vestiges to this ownership group.

From left to right Walter O' Malley, Kay O' Malley, Dearie McKeever Mulvey and James Mulvey

Index

George McLaughlin, 220
George W. Chauncey, **72**
George Washington, **52**, **54**, **152**
Gilded Age, **74**
Ginney Flats, **101**
Gloucester Racetrack, **84**
Gowanus, **52**, **53**, **54**, **61**, **149**, **234**
Gowanus Canal, **52**, **54**, **61**
Grace Nott, 217
Grand Canyon, 153
Grand Central Station, 182
Grantland Rice, 151
Greenwood Cemetery, 216
Greyhound Buses, **136**
Groucho Marx, 165
Gus Abell, **60**, **78**, **81**, **93**, **110**, **111**, **133**, **138**, **142**, **146**, **216**
Hal Janvrin, 186, 191
Hanlon
Ned Hanlon, **111**, **117**, **118**, **120**, **123**, **127**, **128**, **129**, **130**, **131**, **138**, **139**, **142**, **143**
Harry Hooper, 186, 191
Harry Lumley, **99**
Harry M. Stevens, **111**, **179**, **238**
Harry von Der Horst, **87**, **156**
Henry Carter, **134**
Henry Chadwick, **78**, **108**, **111**, **216**
Henry J. Medicus, 130, 156
Henry J. Robinson, **73**

Herbert Casey, 214
Highlanders, 143
Horsefeathers, 165
Houston Street, **132**
Hudson River Broken Stone Company, 157
Hy" Myers, 185
Jake Daubert, 166, 181, 195
Jake Rupert, 143, 161, 193
Jamaica Bay, 97, 157
James Mulvey, 220
James Peebles, **112**
James Sheckard, **99**
Jeff Pfeffer, 183, 185, 186, 190, 191, 195
Jimmy Walker, 196
Joe Doyle
Joseph J. Doyle, **89**
Joe Oeschger, 198, 199
John (Monte) Montgomery Ward
Ward, **66**
John B, Day, **112**
John B. Day, **60**
John Brush, **115**
John Kelly, **112**
John Montgomery Ward, **62**, **71**, **127**, **195**
John Wallace, **73**
Jones. McGinnity and Cross, **130**
Joseph Gilleaudeau,, 221
Joseph J. Doyle, **84**, **89**, **93**, **216**
Judge, 61, 158, 172, 201, 215, 219

New York Herald, **236**, **238**, **239**
New York Mets, **61**, **68**
New York Times, **106**, **112**, **199**, **233**, **234**, **235**, **236**, **237**, **239**
Newport, **87**, **93**, **118**, **138**, **234**
Niblo's Garden, **133**
Nick Young, **99**, **111**
Noah Webster, 161, 203
Orioles
Baltimore Orioles, **87**, **115**, **117**, **126**, **143**
Otto Miller, 204, 211
Park Slope, **52**, **53**, **149**
Patrick Powers, **111**
Pee Wee Reese, 198
Pete Kilduff, 204, 211
Peter Stuyvesant, **132**
Philadelphia, **68**, **93**, **99**, **109**, **111**, **142**, **180**, **198**, **235**
Pigtown, **105**, **148**, **153**, **156**, **162**
Pirates, **127**
Pitkin Avenue, **71**
Players League, **62**, **66**, **68**, **69**, **72**, **81**, **84**, **85**, **168**, **235**
Polo Grounds, **68**, **161**, **179**, **196**
Potter building, **112**, **118**
Powell Street, **71**
Prospect Park, **92**, **105**
Pylon Construction Company, 149
Queens, **133**, **143**

Rainmakers, **94**
Ray Chapman, 206
Reading Rifle, 151
Red Hook, **52**
Redding and Kiddle, **118**
Revolutionary War, **52**
Ridgewood Land and Improvement Company, **72**, **73**
Ridgewood Park, 143
Robert Ward, 169, 170
Rotunda, 159, 163
Rube Marquard, 180, 183, 186, 189, 190, 202, 203, 208, 238
Shannon's Band, 165
Shea Stadium, **68**, **105**, **173**
Sherry Smith
Sherrod Smith, 180, 184, 195, 202, 209, 211
society club, **87**, **133**
Society Club, **87**
SoHo, **132**
Sporting Life, **69**, **109**, **233**, **235**, **236**, **238**
sporting men, **84**
Sporting News, **180**, **237**, **238**
St. Louis Perfectos, **115**
St. Louis Post Dispatch, **234**
Stan Coveleski, 201, 204, 205, 208, 209, 210, 212
Steve McKeever, 156, 158, 216, 217, 218, 219, 220, 237
Sullivan Street, 148
Sutter Avenue, **71**

Chapter Sources &

Notes

Introduction: It seemed obvious to me that in this story about the Dodgers that I would use Charles Ebbets "History of Baseball in Brooklyn" as seen in the *Brooklyn Eagle* January through March of 1913 as my main source for the introduction. Since this is how Ebbets saw pre-Dodger baseball in Brooklyn I thought to follow suit. I summarized what he thought was important. I tried channeling his spirit and essence by culling his thoughts.

Chapter 1 New York Clipper March 4th, 1899, 11. Charles Ebbets "History of Baseball in Brooklyn" Chapter VII. *Brooklyn Eagle* January 18, 1899 *The Brooklyn Daily Eagle* Sat, Apr 07, 1883 page 2.

Chapter 2 New York City Directory of 1883 New York Clipper March 4th, 1899, 11. Charles Ebbets "History of Baseball in Brooklyn" Chapter VII *Brooklyn Eagle* January 18th, 1899.

Chapter 3 *Brooklyn Eagle* January 5th, 1885 page 21. Sporting Life *October 19th, 1884 page 4 New York Clipper March 4th page 11.* New York Times October 21st, 1890 page 2. Sporting Life Oct 11th, 1890.Philip J. Lowry Green Cathedrals

Walker &Company 2006 page 35. *Brooklyn Eagle* Jan 26th, 1913. *Brooklyn Eagle* Dec 7th, 1887. *Sporting Life* Oct 23rd, 1889. Sporting Life Nov 3rd, 1889. *Sporting Life* Dec 25th, 1897. *Sporting Life* Jan 16th, 1891

Chapter 4 *Cincinnati Enquirer* July 16th, 1886 page 1. *St. Louis Post Dispatch* July 17th, 1886 page 10. New York Times July 12th, 1896. *The Brooklyn Union*, Feb 25th, 1871 page 1.

Chapter 5 1850 U.S. Census Providence, Rhode Island. 1860 and 1861 Providence directory. *The New York Times* Dec 25th, 1866 page 2. *The Daily Milwaukee News* Jan 1st, 1867 page 4. *Burlington Free Press* Dec 16, 1873 page 3. *The Sun* Sep 17th, 1876 page 3. *New York Daily Herald* Sep 20th, 1877 page 10. *The Sun* Jan 2nd, 1880 page 4. *Newport Daily News* Fri, Jan 23, 1880 page 2. *Courier-News* Aug 2nd, 1888 page 2. *The Times* Sep 1, 1889 page 11. *The Sun* Feb 4th, 1892 page 3. *Brooklyn Daily Eagle* Jul 28th, 1894 page 2. *The Standard Union* Jan 17th, 1895 page 8. *New York Times* Jan 17th, 1895 page 1. *The World* Jun 7th, 1896 page 22. *Boston Globe* Oct 1st, 1896 page 5. *The Boston Globe* Jan 3rd, 1897 page 32. *The Baltimore Sun* Apr 13th, 1899 page 6. *Brooklyn Citizen* Nov 10th, 1913 page 4.

Chapter 6 The Original Certificate of Association March 9th, 1883. *New York Clipper* March 10th, 1883. *Brooklyn Union* March 5th, 1883.

Chapter 7 I thought it important enough to add the sources right in the chapter as it better showed the debate using them, in my estimation. Also cited New York City Directories.

Chapter 8 *Brooklyn Eagle* Feb 5th, 1861. Old Stone Fort Website. *Gowanus* by Joseph Alexiou New York University Press 2015 page 47, pages 164-166 for Washington Pond and

Chapter 10 "Superfund me!" Fire coverage Brooklyn Eagle various issues from May 16th to June 1st 1899 to follow entire storyline. Indianapolis Journal October 9th, 1887 page 4. Ronald G. Shafer, *When the Dodgers Were Bridegrooms, Gunner McGunnigle and Brooklyn's Back-to-Back Pennants of 1889 and 1890* (Jefferson, North Carolina: McFarland & Company Inc., 2011).

Chapter 9 This chapter is a synthesis of notes and reflections from the following: New York Labor History Association; Great Baseball Revolt; The Rise and the Fall of the 1890 Players League by Robert B Ross: *University of Nebraska Press*, 2016; The Origins of the 1890 Players League by Rob Bauer *Kindle Edition* and the various works of Ethan Lewis on the subject. All were used as grist for the chapter in some fashion.

Chapter 10 *Philadelphia Inquirer* December 4th, 1890 page 3. *Brooklyn Eagle* April 4th, 1897 page 4. *Brooklyn Citizen* February 7th, 1891 page 7. *Brooklyn Citizen* Nov. 13th, 1890 page 6. *Brooklyn Eagle* Nov. 13th. 1890. *Brooklyn Eagle* of February 8th, 1894 on page 8. The Wrong Stuff by John G. Zinn from *manlypastime.blogspot.com*.

Chapter 11 *Sporting Life* January 8th, 1898 page 5. *Brooklyn Times* Mar 2nd, 1898 page 7. *New York Times* January 5th, 1898 page 7. *Brooklyn Eagle* Jan 6TH, 1898 page 16. *Baltimore Sun* Feb 11th, 1899 page 6. *Buffalo Commercial* Jan 8th, 1906 page 1 White Plains Library and Historical Association

Chapter 12 All sources cited directly in the chapter.

Chapter 13 *Brooklyn Eagle* May 1st, 1898 page 18. *Brooklyn Eagle* Mar 24th, 1898. *New York Times* Mar 20th, 1898 page 16. *Brooklyn Eagle* Jan 18th, 1898 *New York Times*. page10. *brooklynballparks.com* and my good friends Andrew Ross and

David Dyte, with whom I contributed to do their fine work on Washington Park 1 and their other Dodger topics.

Chapter 14 *Brooklyn Eagle* Jan 6th, 1898 page 16. New York Times Jan 13th, 1898 page 4. *Brooklyn Times.* March 2nd, 1898. *Sporting Life* Jan 15th, 1898. *Sporting Life* Jan 15th, 1898. *Sporting Life* December 25th, 1897. Summary of Charles Byrne's contributions were freely stolen from fellow SABR member Ronald C. Shafer from his SABR paper on Charles Byrne. I added some clarity about raincheck contributions of Ebbets vs. Byrne. You can't top the tops—so why try? Chadwick Eulogy of Charles Byrne.

Chapter 15 *New York Sun* Jan 9th, 1900 page 5. *Brooklyn Eagle* December 21st, 1898 page 11. The Sun Feb 11th, 1899 page 5. *Brooklyn Eagle* December 28th, 1898 page 23. *Baltimore American* January 3rd page 16.

Chapter 16 Bel Air Road and North Avenue- The First intersection of Beer and Baseball-David B. Stinson 2015. Ned Hanlon Zack Stinson SABR paper. The Sun Feb 11th, 1899 page 5.

Chapter 17 *U.S. Census* of 1850 & 1860 New York Directories of 1850- 1865 *New York Herald* Sep 11th, 1860 page 3. *New York Daily News* Sep 28th, 1941 pages 194-196. Charles Ebbets John G. Zinn Mc Farland 2019 pages 15-19 & 24-35. *Brooklyn Eagle* Jan 18th, 1913 page 23. *Brooklyn Eagle* Mar 1st, 1891 page 8. *Brooklyn Eagle* Jan 2nd, 1898 page 22. The Sun Feb 2nd, 1898 page 4. *Baltimore Sun* Feb 3rd, 1898 page 6. *Brooklyn Eagle* March 1st, 1913 page 23. *Baltimore Sun* Nov 4th, 1907 page 10.

Chapter 18 The Great Game website 1901 American League. Don Johnson & Cindy Thomson SABR paper. Ban Johnson BBHOF website.

Chapter 19 & 21 *Brooklyn Eagle* Jan 3rd, 1912 pages 21-22. *Brooklyn Eagle* Apr 13th, 1913 pages 23-26. *Brooklyn Eagle* April 4th, 1913 page 19. *Brooklyn Eagle* April 6th, 1913 page 1 & 58. *Brooklyn Eagle* Apr 9th, 1913 pages 22-26 Charles Ebbets SABR paper John Saccoman. *New York Tribune* Jan 3rd, 1912 page 8. *New York Tribune* Jan 3rd, 1912 page 8. *Brooklyn Eagle* Feb 1st, 1912 page 22. *Brooklyn Eagle* Jan 10th, 1912 page 23. *Brooklyn Eagle* Feb 10th, 1912 page 1. *Brooklyn Eagle* Feb 19th, 1912 page 7. *Brooklyn Eagle* Feb 4th, 1912 page 43. New York Times Apr 6th, 1913 page 13. *Brooklyn Daily Times* Apr 13th, 1913 page 13. *Brooklyn Eagle* April 5th, 1913 page 1. *New York Times* Apr 6th 1913 pages 58-59. *Brooklyn Eagle* Apr 11th, 1913 page 2. *Brooklyn Eagle* Apr 12th, 1913 page 18. Charles Ebbets John G. Zinn Mc Farland 2019 chapter IX.

Chapter 20 Frank Graham *"The Brooklyn Dodgers"* an informal History Putnam 1945 pages 34-36. "find a grave website" on Steve McKeever. *The Sporting News*, Mar 10th, 1938 page 7. *Brooklyn Eagle* Apr 9th, 1913 page 19. *The Sporting News* November 21st, 1935. *New York Times* Apr 30th, 1925.

Chapter 22 Was the Federal League a Major League? Emil Rothe SABR paper. The Short Shelf life of the Tip Tops-Bowery Boys New York City History. Washington Park III *brooklynparks.com.* my good friends Andrew Ross and David Dyte with whom I contributed to do their fine work on Washington Park history. "Third Major Baseball League Formed". *Chicago Tribune. July 28, 1959. p. 39*

Chapter 23 Washington Park Wall *brooklynparks.com.* my good friends Andrew Ross and David Dyte with whom I contributed to do their fine work on Washington Park history. Before Nathan's there was Feltman's: The history of the Coney Island hot dog Coney Island History by Dana Schultz. The Legacy of Harry M. Stevens - ohiomagazine.com

Chapter 24 *Sporting News* Apr 13th, 1916 page 5. *Brooklyn Eagle* Oct 5th, 1916 page 25. *New York Sun* Sep 22nd, 1916 page 22. *Washington Post* Oct 9th, 1916 page 8. *Brooklyn Eagle* Oct 11th, 1916 page 25. *Sporting Life* Nov 18th, 1916 page 6. *Brooklyn Eagle* Oct 17th, page 6. *Evening World* Oct 4th, 1916 page 12. *New York Tribune* Nov 12th, 1916 page 12. Charles Ebbets John G. Zinn Mc Farland 2019 Chapter XI.

Sun Jul 27th, 1918 page 11. *Brooklyn Eagle* Sep 14th, 1918 page 16. *New York Tribune* Nov 20th, 1918 page 13. *New York Tribune* Aug 30th, 1919 page 10. *Brooklyn Eagle* Jun 13th, 1916 page 22. *New York Tribune* Oct 21st, 1916 page 15. *New York Sun* Jun 24th, 1919 page 2. *Brooklyn Eagle* Jul 6th, 1917 page 1. *Brooklyn Eagle* Sep 24th, 1917 page 1. *Brooklyn Eagle* Jan 9th, 1918 page 20. *New York Sun* Aug 18th, 1919 page 17. *New York Sun* Aug 18th, 1919 page 17. *Brooklyn Eagle* May 5th, 1919 page 18.

Chapter 26 *Brooklyn Eagle* May 12th, 1920 page 67. *Brooklyn Eagle* May 3rd, 1920 page 18. *Brooklyn Eagle* Sep 29th, 1920 page 18. *Brooklyn Eagle* Oct 4th, 1920 page 1. *Brooklyn Eagle* Sep 21st, 1920 page 20. *Brooklyn Eagle* Oct 3rd, 1920 page 64. *Brooklyn Eagle* Oct 6th, 1920 page 22. *Brooklyn Eagle* Oct 8th, 1920 page 24. Larry Mansch, Rube Marquard-The Life and Times of a Baseball Hall of Famer McFarland 1998 pages 183-187. *Brooklyn Eagle* Oct 11th, 1920 page 1. *New York Herald*

Sep 27th, page 8. *Brooklyn Eagle* Oct 10th, 1920 page 1. *Brooklyn Eagle* Oct 11th, 1920 page 20. *Brooklyn Eagle* Oct 13th, 1920 page 22. *Brooklyn Eagle* Oct 21st, 1920 page 20.

Chapter 27 *Brooklyn Eagle* Jun 9th, 1919 page 18. *Brooklyn Eagle* Apr 25th, 1920 page 18. *Brooklyn Eagle* Oct 4th, 1923 page 22. *Brooklyn Eagle* Jul 16th, 1920 page 1. *Brooklyn Eagle* Nov 2nd, 1920 page 26. *Brooklyn Eagle* Feb 15th, 1920 page 24. *Brooklyn Eagle* Apr 10th, 1924 page 26. *Brooklyn Eagle* Mar 2nd, 1925 page 2. *Brooklyn Eagle* Mar 5th, 1925 page 22. *Brooklyn Eagle* Mar 7th, 1925 page 4. *Brooklyn Eagle* Mar 15th, 1925 page 24. *Brooklyn Eagle* Apr 7th, 1920 page 20. *Brooklyn Eagle* Apr 10th, 1925 page 20. *Brooklyn Eagle* Apr 19th, 1925 page 1. *Brooklyn Eagle* Apr 20th, 1925 page 22. *Brooklyn Eagle* May 6th, 1925 page 1. *Brooklyn Eagle* Apr 27th, 1925 page 3. *Brooklyn Eagle* May 25th, 1925 page 1. *Brooklyn Eagle* May 25th, 1925 page 1. *Brooklyn Eagle* Apr 19th, 1925 page 1. *Brooklyn Eagle* Apr 19th, 1925 page 8. *New York Herald Tribune* Apr 22nd, 1925 page 20.

Chapter 25 *New York Times* Feb 25th, 1917 page 24. *Brooklyn Eagle* Jan 24[th,] 1917. *Brooklyn Eagle* Jan 11th, 1918 page 20. *Brooklyn Eagle* Mar 18th, 1917 page 33. *Brooklyn Eagle* Mar 27th, 1917 page 27. *Brooklyn Eagle* Feb 11th, 1917 page 33. *Brooklyn Eagle* Apr 16th, 1917 page 1. *Brooklyn Eagle* Feb 15th, 1918 page 15. *New York Times* Feb 12th, 1918 page 12. *Brooklyn Eagle* Mar 22nd, 1918 page 1. *New York*

Epilogue New York <u>Daily News</u> Sep 28th, 1941 page 194 195 196. Harold Parrott "The Lords of Baseball" Praeger 1976 page 99.

About the Author

Allen Schery has been a Dodger fan since he was in the crib listening to Red Barber and Vin Scully whose voices were on the radio before he knew what they were talking about. Living in the neighborhood it was natural he would become a fan. He knew and met all of the "Boys of Summer" and felt it would never end. 1958 put an end to that dream as they left to go to Los Angeles. Despite that, the imagery of those days never left his head. He started and never stopped collecting Dodger memorabilia. As collector conventions began in Brooklyn, Allen went to every one of them amassing over 250,000 artifacts. When he entered the door dealers rushed to him rather than him seek out artifacts table by table! Many of those artifacts are seen throughout the pages of this book. Pictures were garnered from old newspapers and from various dealers over a 70-year period. Mark Langill, Dodger Team Historian allowed Allen to publish an article in a Dodger Magazine game program in 2008 about Washington Park. That research put him on the road to what became this book. Allen also has restored and collected Corvettes as well. In 1991 he opened the unique Corvette Americana Museum in Cooperstown New York, near the Baseball Hall of Fame. The museum was unusual in that it was designed by the mind of a trained Anthropologist who treated each car as a time-coordinated American artifact surrounded by the sights and sounds of that year featuring music, television, and news slides. Each car was in a time capsule displayed in front of a giant photo mural of a well-known American landmark lit with stage lighting. Allen took all the background photographs. He was given an award for one of the ten best museums in New York State. Other winners included the Guggenheim, Metropolitan Museum of Art along with the Corning and Kodak museums. The Dodgers found him in 1999 and brought him to work on the Dodger Experience Museum at Dodger Stadium in 1999. He also designed the Rose Bowl Millenium Museum in Pasadena as well. Allen. as an Anthropologist, has also written: "the Dragons Breath-The Human Experience" to explain what it means to be human. He is also working on a Dodger Museum as well.

Allen Schery on right in 1953 had already started his Dodger dreams and collection. Mother Paulette and brother Bruce also seen in the picture